BUDDHIST
TALES FOR THE
SOUL

By the same author

Buddhist Tales in Modern Times

Stories of the Soul

BUDDHIST
TALES FOR THE
SOUL

Bhikshu Gyomyo Nakamura

STERLING

STERLING PAPERBACKS
An imprint of
Sterling Publishers (P) Ltd.
A-59, Okhla Industrial Area, Phase-II, New Delhi-110020.
Tel: 26387070, 26386209; Fax: 91-11-26383788
E-mail: mail@sterlingpublishers.com
www.sterlingpublishers.com

Buddhist Tales for the Soul
© 2012, Bhikshu Gyomyo Nakamura
ISBN 978 81 207 6841 3

All rights are reserved.
No part of this publication may be reproduced, stored in a retrieval system or transmitted, in any form or by any means, mechanical, photocopying, recording or otherwise, without prior written permission of the author.

Printed and Published by Sterling Publishers Pvt. Ltd.,
New Delhi-110 020.

Contents

1. Tama – The Temple Cat — 7
2. The Youth and the Hermit — 13
3. The Yogi — 19
4. Maria in London — 24
5. The End of the Dharma Wheel — 30
6. Holy War — 35
7. Ramen Yoshi's Middle Way — 40
8. Ram in the Slums — 46
9. Raju's Dreams — 57
10. The Last Days of Jizō in Japan — 67
11. The Pilgrim Monk — 74
12. Annie's Middle Way — 80
13. Baba and the Dropouts — 84
14. Kuttā – The Dog Saint — 90
15. Following the Wind — 95
16. Kumar – The Travel Guide — 104
17. Dan's Journey — 114

18. Hathī – The Elephant 127
19. The Plight of India's Mice 133
20. Kenchin's Soup (Japanese Minestrone Soup) 139
21. Haruka's Dream 143
22. Fortune Pickles and Curry Rice 154

Tama – The Temple Cat

There was a stray cat called Tama who once lazed around a big temple with his fat, round body and tail in tow.

This temple was for only renunciates – those monks and nuns who had tossed away their old homes to practice here. They had renounced their old lives and so were called renunciates. It was also known to everyone that only renunciates lived in this temple. Tama, in actuality was taken care of in the temple and so he was a kind of renunciate cat, but nobody called him as such. Everyone in the temple had already long thrown away their old lives and had no desires for possessions. There was nobody to look after the cat, so in that sense, Tama was a stray cat.

The master of the temple was quite strict and he completely rejected hierarchy and politically motivated positions, but still the order of seating according to when one had entered the temple was strictly maintained.

This stray cat Tama, was already a senior colleague. The lifespan of a cat to a human is eight years to one. With that calculation in mind he was already an elder. But the master made no mention of cats in the monastic order, so he had an idle existence like air and, as it were, he lived in the temple as an old timer who didn't bother anyone.

Below in the order of seniority was an underling dog called Shiro. Shiro would wag his tail with delight whenever the monks would bang the drums.

Long ago the renunciates would visit the villages banging drums to the delight of the children. The villagers would happily offer money and meals to the renunciates. Their hearts would flutter at the sight of the monks and nuns.

Nowadays they give suspicious looks and coldly ignored them. Shiro wagging his tail became their sole comfort.

"Hearts fluttering" and "tails wagging" is nothing more than a difference in expression between people and dogs. That's why everyone in the temple loved Shiro.

The precinct of the temple was incredibly large and everyone in the temple, like a pack of mice, bustled about as they had to clean both the temple and gardens. Each one worked so hard, but that stray cat Tama, just lazed around.

Originally, a "house cat" had the task of catching mice, but Tama was a "stray cat" and while everyone trained and moved about like a bunch of mice, he had to respect all life and so he never caught a single mouse in his life.

Never to take life was the foremost teaching of the Buddha and in the temple more than taking care of beings they had to observe the precept of never taking life.

Sometimes the temple got so busy that it seemed like they wanted to borrow even the cat's paw for help.

Tama was well aware that humans critically called him a four-legged animal. So, while he had a feeling of wanting to help out, there was a clear policy requiring two hands and two legs. They had to first settle and abolish this issue of discrimination against those with four legs before he could be put to work. That's why he just lazed around. So that stray cat Tama, was always quite idle and had time to think. Now, in explaining the reason for his laziness, he was already quite a philosopher. Still, everyone in the temple loved him.

Seeing Tama lazing around prompted a sigh of relief after the monks finished strict and difficult practices like long meditation retreats. An existence of idleness, permitted and even encouraged, enriched the hearts of everyone. Each one in the temple would pat him on the back and he would purr signalling another day of idleness – his daily practice – and fawn over everyone.

Everybody in the temple had the daily practice of reciting the title of the Lotus Sutra and every morning and evening they would recite. *Namu-Myo-Ho-Renge-Kyo*.Tama announced his idleness through purring. Tama for a long time had been watching everyone in the temple.

Each one had been training so hard and the large precincts had become splendid and beautiful beyond recognition.

It was in the last ten years that the important places of worship had increased to about ten more. Tama's worry was that along with that increase everyone had grown ten years older. The faithful devotees had also grown ten years older and the younger people did not really come to the temple so much anymore. Tama thought it would be nice if the children came to visit more. So in the middle of the night he would pray to the statues of Buddha, the Bodhisattvas and Gods in the temple grounds. For a cat that was quite idle most of the time, the only thing he could do was pay his respect to the enshrined Buddha and deities and pray to them.

"The Buddha is always there for those who train tirelessly. In bitter and sad times, in the times when one seeks to give something to society – parents and teachers cannot help, but if I should pray to the Buddha, I will surely receive aid and I can become a person capable of helping the people."

Today again when nobody was looking, Tama went around the temple grounds and offered his prayers. Tama's eyes were different from those of people as he could see the light of the Buddha in the darkness. Shiro was afraid of the dark and barked, but Tama without anyone knowing said his prayers in the light of the Buddha.

"In those places the people tirelessly pay their respect and worship, the Buddha manifests. Though it be bitter and sad, and parents and teachers may not understand, the Buddha most certainly comes to aid us. Then one may become someone who is capable of helping others."

Tama was definitely a temple cat. He didn't just laze around. Today again without people knowing or noticing he continues his rounds. No matter how many sites of worship there were, he was fine with it. That's because he didn't have two legs, but four and that made the burden half. He knew the shortcut of animal trails. Just as there was a trail for humans taught by the Buddha, so too was there a trail for stray cats. Tama passed through those animal trails which were trails leading to places of worship around the huge temple grounds. Maybe in his next life he will be reborn as a human who will protect the temple. Then by the prayers of the stray cat Tama, some children who had come to visit before became adults, and Tama had been reborn as a little monk and was affectionately taken care of by them. This is karma and in monastic life so many souls go around and are reborn. They are firmly rooted into the temples and in life and death they are seldom parted from it.

Comment:

This story is a common phenomenon in Buddhist temples and Shintō shrines because the health department of Japan kills stray dogs and cats if they are found within city limits. Many people when they cannot take care of a cat or a dog, offer it to a temple or shrine and in other cases many stray dogs and cats seek asylum in temples. Even ancient Japanese Buddhist books mention about cats and dogs training together with humans.

The Youth and the Hermit

Many many years ago there lived a hermit in a deep cave in the mountains of Tibet. It was so long that he lived there and he did not even know for how long he had been there. From the village one had to walk more than a day to reach there, and from the town for more than three days.

Sometimes the villagers and townspeople would see the hermit here and there much to their surprise which led to a lot of chatter amongst them. It was as if with some strange paranormal ability he manifested himself here and there. The people of the town and village greatly respected him both as a mountain guardian God and as a representative of the Buddha.

Once a youth ventured into the mountains. This youth carried a blazing inferno in his mind and unaware of what to do he ran into the mountains seeking relief. The power of that inferno inside him was so strong, that anyone who would come close was burned. Many people had already been burned. That's why he once reflected on this and in the middle of the winter jumped into the Indus river. It was indeed cold even just recollecting it. He jumped in with a splash and fainted. The villagers saved him. It was at that time he realized that perhaps the blaze in the body and the mind are different. He started to think over the difference between the two fires within him.

The youth walked to the villagers and asked some questions. "How is the inferno of the mind different from that of the body?" "Why is everyone burned by the blaze inside me?" "Why does everyone run away?" Though he asked them, the villagers just looked at him timidly without getting too close and did not respond to his questions. The villagers whispered amongst themselves that the hooligan youth had snapped at last. Some time later the youth found the mountain hermit after being told by a decrepit old man that the hermit would probably know the answers to his questions.

The youth, tired and wheezing, prostrated himself before the hermit and asked his questions. "The fire in my mind burns bright red and I always burn those around me despite that the fire in my body is the same as others. Won't you teach me the difference between the fire of the body and the fire of the mind? If you teach me I will do anything you want and will never forget your teachings."

The truth is that the youth was carrying a fire in his heart, too hot to bear and was burdened with the burns from within it. Thus, he genuinely sought help from the hermit. The youth that the hermit had been waiting for had finally arrived and finally he felt relieved. No matter how much he was called hermit and thought of as a seemingly supernatural being, he was already quite aged and started to feel it. Gathering firewood, drawing water and preparing food by himself had become troublesome. Now, this strange youth had showed up. The hermit thought to himself, "All right."

In actuality the hermit did not understand any difference between the blaze of the mind and the blaze of the body. For him the mind and body were the same and he knew this through many years of experience. So he replied, "Do not worry yourself. The time when you understand will surely come. Until such time train yourself here in the cave. Gather firewood, draw water, prepare meals and serve me. You will then certainly know the answer." The youth was overjoyed as he thought the solution could really be as easy as that. From thereon everyday, the youth would go around the mountain to gather firewood, draw water and prepare meals. The hermit was quite relieved. He would always sit in the sun and with a smile watch the youth.

However, the villagers did not smile upon him at all. They were scared of him and they kept their distance.

Just seeing him they would frown and quickly make their escape. So, the youth became happy. When he became happy a certain kind of strength emerged.

On both rainy and windy days, everyday without exception, he would gather firewood, draw water and prepare meals for the hermit and this continued onward. There was no need to toil searching for an answer to his questions. He completely forgot his old worries and doubts.

One day while sitting atop a rock in a canyon and watching a school of fish in a clear stream he suddenly thought to himself, "Why am I here? What am I doing here?" He recollected having risked his life coming here and the problems he had been dealing with before. "Right... How is the blaze of the mind different from the blaze of the body? I didn't know and ended up coming here."

Looking back in his past he realized that the blazes of body and mind had already become one. It was like the soft brilliance of the sun setting at dusk. It felt like he could express this feeling in an utterance not unlike a *mantra*.

"Ah... Hm..."

The youth no longer felt like he was drowning in confusion as before. He went to the hermit. He was swaying back and forth relaxing in the sunshine.

The youth discussed with the hermit what he had thought, noticed and realized. The hermit completely opened his half-open eyes and with a warm smile remarked, "Ah... Hm..." and nodded his head. It was then that in the space between the youth and hermit a bright light appeared which flowed into the youth's heart. The hermit suddenly sighed and chuckling suddenly vanished with a sound like a tree hitting the ground.

The hermit who had been living some hundreds of years which he himself had not kept track of, had conveyed to the youth the same important thing he had taught to people and vanished.

The youth sobbed and called out the hermit's name. He finally got up and washed his face with the water he had drawn earlier from the river. He looked down into the tub of water and it was not his face but the hermit's that he was looking at. He panicked and scanned himself over. The youth had become the hermit.

The hermit had not really vanished, but was inside the youth. Again for many decades he would be able to convey his teachings to the people. The people in the mountains of Tibet believed that the hermits whenever and wherever can live extremely long lives and convey onto them many blessings.

In Tibet, the wisdom of the Buddha and the teachings of enlightenment flow like this and are conveyed to the people.

The youth who had become the hermit without ever getting close to the villagers would again wait for some strange youth in the future to come to him and all the while convey onto the people blessings and cultivate himself in spiritual training.

Comment:

This story was an adaptation of the Lotus Sūtra chapter entitled Devadatta combined with the Tibetan hermit tradition. Taking care of one's master is one of the most important practices. That is the main aim I wish to emphasize in this story. People in the present era try to understand Buddhism through philosophical ways with too much information and books around them. However, people sometimes forget how to serve their masters and gain wisdom without words, letters or language.

The Yogi

In the steep mountains of Tibet, there was a spiritual practitioner called yogi meditating in a cave. He did not cut his hair or wash himself. He wore only a single robe.

High on the Tibetan plateau, there were many wild animals. The yogi lived no different than the wild animals. The only difference was that he used fire to prepare his food and that he meditated and prayed.

At times villagers and devotees would climb the steep mountain road to bring food to him. He received the food without any word and expressed his gratitude by reciting a *sutra*. He would then retire to the cave and again devote himself to further days of meditation and prayer.

The yogi's friends included birds, deer, rabbits, snow leopards, wild goats and ibex. The animals all probably knew well that the yogi would do no harm to them. Many would cautiously approach him. Just being around him felt like one was in the sunshine and so at times they would gather around the yogi and pass the time in his presence.

The yogi was praised as a saint by people on the street. However, the one in the cave had once been betrayed by those he loved and believed in. Being utterly exhausted he had resolved to kill himself and holed up in the cave.

The wounds of the heart are different from the body and do not heal so easily. The yogi could not live with hatred. It was because it was against the Buddha's teachings of compassion. He also knew that though he might injure his body he would heal his heart.

Love and trust those who the yogi had loved – friends, wealth and relatives were all washed away in a giant flood of hatred. When all the things he had clung to were gone, a yogi of austerities was born. He represented all the pains of those people who had been born into the world.

The yogi felt that perhaps it would be good to go down into the streets and spread the Buddha's teachings, but he realized that the wounds of his heart were still deep and the light shining behind him was still insufficient.

In his dreams many delusions of marketplace sounds, the smells of delicious foods and beautiful serene women would all appear. However, when he took a moment to look at himself, there were just his ragged clothes, emaciated body and the space of the empty cave.

Sometimes when he was in meditation, the Buddha and his disciples along with some heavenly maidens would swoop down and teach with a beautiful melody and his body would float up into the sky. His mind would then ascend into space.

When he was young his teacher often told him, "Don't pray for yourself. Pray for others, society and the world." Because he was time and time again told to do it, he revolted against it. Now, the object of his prayers naturally widened.

Until the yogi had lost everything he felt fed up with his own stupidity that he had not noticed and realizing this stupidity in itself was the reason of the existence. He directed the power of his prayers toward the world. Now, he spoke to nobody except the animals, but when his wounds of the heart had finally healed he would surely descend the mountain.

From the yogi's body light poured out. Society was purified by it. Indeed without expressing many words, the *mantras* the yogi recited helped heal the hearts of others.

In Tibet, someone who had suffered many wounds of the heart and holed up in a cave for spiritual practices was able to turn around his pain to use as medicine for others to heal their wounds. The Tibetans underwent the struggles of time mutually helping one another – patient became doctor, the doctor became patient, disciple became master and master became disciple.

The yogi still continues his practices to this day. He will certainly descend the mountain one day and appear before everyone.

Comment:

This story is based on the tale of Milarepa, the famous Tibetan yogi. He was betrayed by his relatives and fellow villagers and as a result turned to practicing *dharma*. Similar stories exist in Japan and in this century depression is one of the most pressing issues. Even people in ancient times had similar conditions, but they stayed in mountains and practiced *dharma*. Afterwards, they would return to society with the wisdom they had attained.

Maria in London

Maria was born on the Mediterranean island of Cyprus. The island of Cyprus is situated between Turkey and Greece and due to the constant problems there, Maria moved together with her parents to London.

The people of Cyprus were Christian and they often gave girls the name of Maria, the name of the mother of Christ, who in English is known as Mary.

Parted from their homeland, the Mediterranean and living in a city with many Asians, these people came to a small area of London. They focused more on images of Mary than on those of Christ in their prayers. It was because looking at images of Mary made them remember more about their country down south in the Mediterranean sea.

In this city without much belief in anything the people of Cyprus worshipped Mary just like the local Chinese people worshipped Guanyin, or as the Indians called him Avalokiteśvara. This was the only way to tolerate the sad and cold winter and warm the hearts in the freezing rain and wind of London.

Maria in just such an environment as a girl named after Mary passed her childhood years. Maria, named after Mary, lived her childhood years in this kind of our environment. How would you feel if you were named after Guanyin? It might feel a bit embarrassing at first, however, it is possible that you might start to appreciate it. When Maria was called Mary, she would always feel a bit unnerved and then later go before the image of Mary and say, "Please send a warm wind! Please warm our hearts! To that person who called me Mary, envelope them in your light!"

One day in a corner of the library she happened to come across a strange book called *The Questions of King Milinda*. More than two thousand years ago the Indian King Ashoka had sent a teacher to transmit the *dharma* and a message of peace to King Milinda.

Maria had often wondered if the Chinese neighbour's Guanyin was not the same as her family's Mary. They were certainly different in a sense, but thinking about the families both had the same kind of feeling when they revered their respective images. They were different, but if the sense of belief and prayer were the same, then gradually they would come to have the same appearance for Maria. It was perhaps because of the sensitivity she had been born with and that she was named after a holy figure.

From thereon she started going to the library everyday.

At last she found the Buddha with a face similar to the Gods of Cyprus and Greece. It was a Buddha from Gandhāra looking quite like a Greek and many other similar looking Bodhisattvas sitting beside him.

Maria suddenly felt some shutter at the depths of her heart – a very strange feeling of nostalgia and remembrance.

She knew that at the British Museum, which was close to her house, they had a Buddha statue from Gandhāra. She started going there everyday. She would pull up a chair in front of it and spend much of her time just sitting there. Her parents started to worry. Other girls of her age did nothing but play around all day, but seeing Maria going to the museum everyday they thought something was up as they started to sense a kind of holy glow about her.

Today again she was waiting on the steps of the museum to open in the early morning. The morning sun in London's winter was beginning to peep through the buildings in the eastern sky. The fallen autumn leaves danced around and came closer and closer.

Maria then repeated the same prayer to Mary as before. "Please send a warm wind! Please warm our hearts! To that person who called me Mary, envelope them in your light!"

Maria was reassured. A warm wind and light from the east came her way. She thought to herself that just as the sun seemingly climbs from the east, if her prayers to Mary went to the eastern country, they would surely be answered.

On the same day she found a Buddha statue in the Gandhāra collection with the description of parinirvāṇa written underneath. It was an image of the Buddha passing away. It was also written that he was eighty years old when he passed into parinirvāṇa.

Maria strangely begun thinking to herself, "What is the difference between compassion and love?"

Light from the stained glass ceiling above suddenly shown down onto the Buddha statue before her. The various colours of blue, red, green and yellow gently bathed the statue. She realized that Christ, who died in his thirties, was love and Buddha, who died in his eighties, was compassion. Love was the twinkling of light and compassion was the light itself. She further thought that perhaps her father, always busy with work, was love and her grandfather, who had come from Cyprus and everyday smiling treated her so well, was compassion. Mary, whose life experience was longer than Christ, perhaps came closer to compassion as well.

Maria decided that she herself would follow love until around the age of thirty, and then compassion from there. Again she said to herself, "Please send a warm wind! Please warm our hearts! To that person who called me Mary, envelope them in your light!"

After graduating school, Maria would certainly travel to eastern countries and search out the origin of the light, collecting it and bringing the light back to the dark winter of London.

First there would be the kindling and then the light.

Comment:

This story compares the Maria worship in Europe with the Avalokiteśvara worship in Asia. It also alludes to pre-Christian connections between Buddhism and Greek civilization. This was my personal experience during my stay in England in 1980.

The End of the Dharma Wheel

There was once a wheel about as tall as a child that went round and round India's country roads. Its master was a big white ox and slowly the cart carried heavy cargo on the roads. The wheel was always proud of itself, puffing its chest out as it was made from the wood of the great Bodhi Tree.

The Buddha had attained enlightenment underneath the Bodhi Tree. Buddha's teaching was said to be like a wheel and as such the wheel became a symbol of Buddhism and therefore the idea of the Wheel of the Dharma was born. The Buddha's sermons came to be called the turning of the

Wheel of the Dharma. Indeed, everyday the wheel went round and round preaching the *dharma*.

Some two-thousand five-hundred years ago, long before Buddha statues came to exist, Buddha was portrayed as the Dharma Wheel in paintings and in engravings. The people paid reverence to the Dharma Wheel.

In the middle of the Indian flag also there is a wheel. It is a foundation for the hearts of Indians as it symbolises their identify. That's why the wheel is so proud of itself, puffing its chest out. It goes round and round the country's roadways.

The Buddha said that the ultimate teaching was like a cart pulled by a great white ox. That's why the wheel had its nose up in the air. "Does a wheel have a chest or nose?" Of course not, nevertheless, it still "puffed its chest out" and "had its nose up in the air." The wheel once had an accident when its nose was broken and its chest pierced.

There was once a black dog named Kuro who would run around and through the wheel wagging his tail. But one day he was run over by a truck.

The wheel came to hate his relative tyre the rubber tyre. The difference the speed between them was different and they could not speak to one another. The wheel could only speak and think when it was going round and round. The rubber tyre would speed down the middle of the road with stinking fumes behind it.

If the ox-cart was there you would hear *beep... beep... beep...* and it would be forced out of the way.

Finally his irreplaceable friend was killed by a tyre.

The wheel's ancestors back in the time of the Buddha were once compared to the teaching of the Buddha, but nowadays wheels that killed beings had increased in number. This wheel, originally made from a mighty tree, filled with anger and sorrow wept with the sound of creaking.

The wheel did not just carry people and things, but revealed to people the stream of life and the spirit – together with the strength of the ox it spoke to people of cyclic existence. Now, even in India such ox-carts were becoming less in number. The wheel realized that it and the ox were the last of their kind. Trucks and cars went by at dizzying speeds. People too were also really dizzy.

With the ox already quite old and the wheel weeping with a creaking sound, one day the wheel snapped and the ox tumbled over hitting his head on a stone. Both of them died. The two had certainly fulfilled their mission of being the great white ox-cart as described by the Buddha, but nobody understood this and unfortunately it was just one old black dog that ever did and he was run over by a tyre. The day the ox-cart died was on the full moon in May of 1998 – Buddha's birthday. It was also the day when India conducted a nuclear weapon's test.

The value of the wheel's existence hit the dust when the nuclear weapon's experiment was carried out. It was the shock to it that it broke.

On that night the cart was enveloped in golden light and it ascended to the full moon as it retired from the position of turning the Dharma Wheel. Its life ended in this world and its spirit became the great white ox-cart that would carry the heavens. From that day onward, the wheels of India were just wheels. The ox-carts were just ox-carts. The legendary great white ox-cart had tossed India away. There would be no more Dharma Wheel to reveal teachings on the roadways. As the speed of wheels became faster and faster, the end of humanity came closer and closer.

There might be a way of averting such destruction if we slow down to the speed of an ox-cart. If such a thing should really happen, then the wheel will become a Dharma Wheel and it will reveal the cycling of the spirit and be the great white ox-cart that carries the burdens of humanity.

Comment:

The Dharmachakra is an icon of Buddhism as well as a symbol for the Republic of India. Present day India is now rapidly developing and both India and Pakistan have tested nuclear weapons. Both countries became nuclear states. This short story reminds us of the non-violent independent movement of Mahatma Gandhi and cautions us about the present situation.

Holy War

Farooq was born on a houseboat on a lake in Kashmir. Being born on the water is quite rare compared to other places in the world, but there in Kashmir many people are born, live and die on the water, living a life like the water reeds.

It was a place just as beautiful as a pleasure garden on land, but just as the houseboat rode along water, times changed. People asked, "Are we India? Or are we the spiritual Islamic kingdom Kashmir?"

At the same time Pakistan called to them with a sweet voice. Sixty years passed on the turbulent waters of politics and everyone felt seasick.

Farooq in his youth was an Indian. Kashmir was also Indian. However, he had set his heart on dying in a nation of Allah. In order to continue as such and to be able to risk his life he constantly recited the Qur'an, prayed and made oaths promising his loyalty.

In his young mind he truly believed without any hesitation Islam to be a kingdom comprising everything from ideas of nationhood, religion, society and culture.

He understood that a nation administers the government and functions with laws, religion administers the mind, society aids the lives of people and culture cultivates art and temperament, but thinking about it all made him feel scattered and uncertain from within. When he thought about what he truly was, he was a child of God and as such he vowed in his heart to die a pure death in Jihad or holy war. That was the sole stable norm in a situation of instability. Holy war or Jihad – it meant fighting in the name of God.

His grandfather Amin often thought of his grandson Farooq and it pained his heart. Fighting in itself is fighting with one's own heart. After living over seventy years he thought perhaps maybe fighting humanity's various miseries and sorrows was the true Jihad. This was something he understood after he started fighting with the fear of death.

Farooq's grandfather, Amin had gone on Hajj once. He was respected as an elder who had gone on the pilgrimage to Mecca before.

The youth Farooq was upset by having to almost walk a tightrope between being branded a terrorist by the government and being devoted to his religion.

Long ago in the houseboat, a newly wed Hindu couple would come everyday. Other times there would be Hindu visitors who would stay over just like family. Besides two or three months of the winter it was always a lively home.

Quite a few movies were filmed there, and Farooq always looked forward to seeing the actresses. He was able to sell souvenirs to all the foreign visitors. Nobody ever made fun of Islam or tried to get anyone to convert.

On seeing such an amiable and lively environment Amin, Farroq's grandfather would be in a state of confusion, and so Amin could not at all understand the whole idea of holy war.

Amin would face Mecca and pray everyday. He felt an angel had been dispatched and that his time to be invited to paradise was soon coming.

One day Amin came to understand the meaning of Jihad and holy war. It was a war between Gods. It was a kind of conflict in the heavens. It had nothing to do with how many believers there were amongst humanity because they were yet to be actually residing in heaven.

Mankind had to live together as brothers. A human could not become God and so they could not speak of God's name.

Amin often asked God, "If I am invited to paradise, I will fight as Allah's warrior there. I will devote my life to this. Please also help Farooq. Holy war is a war in heaven. It is not a war on earth. Please make Kashmir once again a paradise on Earth!"

Today Amin, the elder who once went on Hajj, prayed for Kashmir.

Recently, Farooq had come to fight with his own heart. The closer one came to God, the more difficult the war of the heart became and further one went away from actual conflict.

Comment:

This is a story about political issues in Kashmir valley. I stayed in Kashmir state in 1979 and I have a lot of attachment to the people of Kashmir.

Ramen Yoshi's Middle Way

"Ramen Yoshi" wasn't actually his name originally. Day in and day out he would always dish out large bowls of noodle soup called ramen to the customers and he did this for so long that people started to associate him with it so much that he earned the name Ramen Yoshi.

Yoshi had done some strict training up in the mountains, studied to become a priest but became a ramen shop owner. Every evening at seven o'clock he opened, shop and closed at five in the morning. He was something of a night owl.

At the temple he would start training in the morning with ice cold water being poured over him. Where as he was exposed to hot steam from boiling pots of soup in the restaurant in the middle of the night.

In the temple he had lived among people conducting themselves in a very solid and refined way. On the contrary, presently he was among people who were either half drunk or completely wasted.

Yoshi was once on a pilgrimage to India and felt the vast extreme difference between Japan and India in his skin which changed his life extremely.

Trying to go from one extreme to another; he thought maybe he would attain the true middle way. His training of long, pure mental cultivation was possible because he was not able to hear everyone's woes and worries.

Still, because nobody really understood that he was treated like a weirdo.

Burning the midnight oil was a way to get close to the darkness of humanity. Trying to shine some light into the darkness you had to enter the darkness, but sometimes you got sucked into it, and now Yoshi was feeling exhausted from it.

In the middle of the night when people would try to satisfy their loneliness, they would confuse the emptiness of their hearts as being an emptiness of the stomach and would come to eat ramen.

It was the time when right before sobering up you would feel a complete vacuum in the mind as you were pulled back into reality.

People didn't really come to eat ramen, but rather they came looking to rely on the light of Yoshi's heart.

Flies and other bugs seek the radiant light of a light bulb and the people here too sought the radiant light of the human heart in the midnight glow of the ramen shop and from there they would warm their own hearts.

However, Yoshi had recently been feeling that the radiance of his own heart had been fading.

The light he had stored in his spirit was draining away like a battery becoming low. Burning that midnight oil meant that he was far away from the sun, so he couldn't recharge himself in the sunlight.

His wife's name was Tomo-chan, but this wasn't her real name either. In Japanese a friend is called *tomodachi*, and she always made friends with anyone and everyone, so they called her Tomo-chan. Tomo-chan's problem was that she had to shout to everyone while smiling, "Welcome!" She always had to keep shouting, "Welcome!", while smiling in order to continue being called Tomo-chan or friend.

Tomo-chan before getting married had been working at a French restaurant. It was one of those upscale, classy restaurants where prim and proper people with a touch of haughtiness frequented for dinner and couples chatted completely ignoring the food.

In a complete reversal from when she wore a cute little outfit, conducted herself in a proper modest manner and presented a classy appearance, now she shouted, "One order of ramen coming up!"

At the restaurant it was busiest at the day during the lunch hour, but at two in the morning when the bars shut down for the night, their shop was flooded with customers.

She used to see nothing but beautiful, prim and proper customers, but in her present days it was all completely wasted drunken customers.

Both of them having gone from one extreme to another were trying to open the doors to their souls. It was then coming to the time to search for that road right smack in the middle of extremes.

People often move forward while denying the things that pull them back and so when they really completely deny things they inevitably have to turn back despite having gone forward.

The trip that Yoshi and Tomo-chan had undertaken in their hearts applies to everyone. The two of them in order to open the doors to their souls had to do a complete reversal in life. Now, from the wisdom gained from these two experiences they were looking for the road of the middle way.

What exactly is this road of the middle way?

There are people who do various casual jobs. Everyone passes through their own individual experiences and their job becomes a job for life. They work in various places and at various positions. They have their own wisdom from the job and their own realizations. That assembly is the

Buddha's compassion and maybe realization itself. Those who have found a mission in life and a job where they can devote themselves to others are probably Bodhisattvas.

Now, Yoshi and Tomo-chan both lived their own experiences and were looking for a new way. For that there was now no need to do anything different from what they were doing. They had become people with greater magnitude than most others, so they could do anything – they had already passed the stage of always wondering what they wanted to do or who they wanted to become.

You can judge what people or society is looking for or what right now is needed and have that capacity to do anything. You can say, "Yeah, I can do anything!"

Now, Yoshi and Tomo-chan were preparing the soup stock for the day. It's a secret recipe made with all kinds of experiences, joys, sorrows and pains, and seasoned with the Buddha's compassion.

On everyone's street there is probably a ramen shop owner with the same soup stock.

Comment:

Ramen is the soul food of Japan and common fare. In metropolitan cities you can find ramen shops that are open 24/7. People get hungry in the middle of night or even find themselves lonely and seek out a ramen restaurant. This story explains the Middle Path of Buddhism.

Ram in the Slums

Many people from within India went to the capital New Delhi in search of work. The poor people arrived with literally just the shirts on their backs and settled down in the slums.

The slums were situated on what was once an open space owned by the government. They had originally planned to build a park, but before you knew it, little huts sprung up all over. They had plans to take down the little domiciles, but right at the election time all the residents became valuable voters. The local powerful candidate put a lot of pressure on the residents to vote. He became a member of parliament. The places on land the people occupied were guaranteed as theirs. Everything was carried out according to the plan.

There was no rent to be paid as it was a government land. If any rent was contemplated by the politicians, the people would announce their rights. There were also no official electricity services, so people stole electricity from the power lines. They just handed some money over to an official who turned a blind eye to whole matter.

There were also no water services as it was government land, so people had no water. That's why a "humanitarian aid van" would come by and provide water to the residents who handed over a bit of cash to the driver.

Now, of course there was the law, but the officials conducted their deals in private so as to avoid risking their necks.

There were also no cement roofs as this was government land. They were really just temporary pre-fabricated homes. The people would pile up old bricks for walls. For the roof they would set up a wooden frame and attach a plastic tarp to it.

Once a year some important official would come to inspect everything. The residents would have to make due without electricity for just a little while until the inspection was over and done with.

People had to pick the right winner every time there was a change in government. For the residents, political thought was quite a simple matter of being on the winning side. Still, if they were mistaken in their judgement, they would end up homeless on the street, so they had to exercise extreme caution in their judgement of politics.

The officials were also masters as this was government land. Although, the residents paid half price for their utilities, it all became bonuses for the officials.

So, it was in the middle of town and moreover, everything was half-priced. As long as you just lived without giving much thought to outward appearances, it was a city.

Ram was born in just such a slum. Ram's father was a rickshaw puller. His mother had a job of cleaning up garbage in the train station. Ram went to the elementary school under a bright blue sky. They did not actually have a building for the school, so everyone just sat on the ground and were taught by volunteer wives.

The school had one group in the morning and one in the evening. Ram went to the morning group.

When school was over he had to go to work. His job was going through the garbage his mother gathered and picking out useful articles to be sold to the junk dealers. His mother was a temporary day worker for the rail company, so all the trash was tossed out at once and she had no chance to go through it.

However, for Ram and other such people and also for the junk dealers, it was a mountain of gems.

Many newspapers and magazines were discarded in the trains. There were also juice containers, plastic bags, leftover food, single-use travel items and so on – anything and everything could be recycled.

Ram saw all the different kinds of garbage coming through India and so came to knew well, the size of the country.

There were newspapers of various languages, leftover foods of various flavours, different types of peculiar things. There were also, as it were, the people who threw these things away like garbage. There were plenty of things that could be used with a bit of repair, but they were still tossed away as garbage.

Ram was of the mind that fishing through garbage was far more educational than studying at school.

He would use his head and think, "What is this? How could I recycle it? Would the junk dealer buy it from me?"

Ram's sandals were made from old tyres. Ram's mother had made his clothes from foreign aid supplies. She took them in a bit to make them smaller for Ram. Ram's toy was a broken old toy motorcycle he picked up in the garbage. His textbook was the old textbook of one of his teacher's kids.

The door, window and fan in Ram's house were all procured from the junk dealer who had acquired such items from a demolition site.

From the perspective of someone in a developed country, they were quite ecologically friendly, but in India they were just plain poor.

Here, raw garbage was processed by the cow. The job of cleaning the toilet was left to the pig. Everyone had the seemingly magical ability to turn garbage into something useful.

Everybody knew that all material things had some kind of value and function. That's why they didn't necessarily see value in money, but in various objects. Ram studied this everyday.

Ram's family lived right beside the train track opposite the station. In other countries, this would be a prime quality real-estate, but here, because the trains were loud and people did their business right beside the tracks, it was the most undesirable place to live.

On the other hand, it was one minute to Delhi Station with a toilet and water tap for washing trains right nearby, so in a sense it was the ideal place to live what with being a one-minute commute to work complete with a shower.

Ram's father was a rickshaw puller which was the most common job for anyone in his family who came from the state of Bihar to do in the capital.

There was no set number of people to ride the rickshaw. Once there were about five people riding the rickshaws. One could also pile on a lot of luggage. But recently, as the number of cars on the road increased and jobs decreased, regulated roadways and traffic laws started and as a result work picked up again as driving became a hassle. That's because a rickshaw could go right into the middle of the bazaar while a car could not.

Ram's father had a worry about meeting the cops and being beaten on the rear. The cops did not consider Ram's father to be human – rather they thought of him a cow or a horse. It was because in the traffic laws the role of the rickshaw pullers was ambiguous.

People would pile on their luggage and get off at the station because cars could not get to the same destination, but they could get there by rickshaw.

There was no engine installed on the rickshaw, so it was able to pass freely into the bazaar, but the cops would praise the rickshaw like it was some kind of a fabulous car and they would have to be given bribes. The cops were in charge of managing traffic and they treated rickshaws just like they were chasing away wild cows or carts. The rickshaw pullers were struck and shouted at. If you were disobedient, you couldn't pass. You just had to remain silent like a cow or horse to pass through.

In the beginning Ram's father's pride had been hurt and he flared up at the cops resulting in a badly injured black eye. The disobedience was surprising even for the cops. It appeared that a stray dog had attacked him or a cat suddenly went wild on him. His disobedience was so unacceptable that the cops felt the need to beat him down to the ground with their batons. If they hadn't, then the rickshaw pullers might all freely run around the bazaar and chase away pedestrians.

It was always a matter of the distinction between strong and weak, deciding victory and defeat. That's why for idle pedestrians the rickshaw was advantageous. The puller could look down on people from a high position. Even in a collision it didn't qualify as a traffic accident because there was no engine.

Categorically speaking, Ram's father was not a victim. For the pedestrians he was the authority who made them scatter on the streets. That's why if a pedestrian was struck they would go into a frenzy and kick a stray dog. If a stray dog went into a frenzy it would chase a pig. But, the pig would be lost in a daze while gorging itself.

This was for all intents and purposes the formation of an "orderly society".

Ram's dream was to ride the train and go to the ocean. When he did ride the train it was back to Bihar. Though, the ocean was somewhat close to his father's hometown, Ram couldn't ride the train to Calcutta where he could go see the ocean.

Ram enjoyed dreaming about his future. At the station he saw so many kinds of people getting on and off trains, so he could see all kinds of jobs. He specially liked jobs where people wore uniforms. The train conductors, stewards, officers, soldiers and restaurant waiters all wore uniforms and seemed to have some great role to play in a large group where they were not single individuals. He just didn't care for the cops who beat and harassed his father.

That was really the only thing Ram, who was born in a slum that could easily be blown away at any moment with the wind, could really rely on.

After giving birth to Ram his mother became ill and was told by the doctor that she could no longer become pregnant again, so Ram was a single child.

Ram's mother always started off the day with a prayer to God.

In slums, there was really nothing else to rely on besides God. There was no social safety net for society. If you became ill then you fell into a pitiful condition. She always prayed for the health of her family.

She would fast on days with a full moon for her family. She would also fast an entire week for her family in November. She never ate fish or meat. She thought that it was because of their bad luck that they came to live in such a slum, and that she didn't want to use up anymore merit in this life than she had to. She prayed everyday.

"God, let us live this day without any problems."

"Today please protect Ram and his father. If something should happen to them, I will be the victim. So, please take care."

Ram started to pray together with her. This was because he thought that the figure of his mother praying was the most beautiful thing as it felt divine. He also looked forward to receiving treats from the priest in the temple.

The priest was also from the same state of Bihar. This area of the slum was inhabited entirely by families from Bihar, who mostly were rickshaw pullers. One night they put their efforts together to build a concrete temple and enshrined a statue of God in it. They started their prayers the next morning.

"God, descend from the heavens!"

"God, descend from the heavens!"

They continued singing this throughout the day.

The official from the government didn't lift a finger. He believed that if he destroyed or removed the image there would surely be a punishment, so the only concrete building in the whole slum was able to become a permanent temple.

They also arranged for a priest from their homeland to come. The families took turns cooking meals and offering it to him.

The priest was Hindu, but as he came from Bihar, the original homeland of Shakyamuni Buddha, he often spoke about the Buddha.

It was because theirs was an entirely different environment, time period, lifestyle so entirely divorced from rural life, that the ordinary stories he would have told in the countryside just wouldn't help people in these circumstances.

He thought that perhaps Shakyamuni's teachings, which had a quality of transcending different environments, time periods and people would work. They all believed Shakyamuni was the incarnation or *avatar* of their God Vishnu, so there was no sense of unease at all. The Bihar people were always discriminated against in Delhi anyway, so Shakyamuni was their only refuge.

It was because in India's history Shakyamuni is the greatest Indian and also because he spent most of his life living in Bihar.

Ram came to look forward to listening to the priest's stories.

At school, under the blue sky, it was just reading and writing. With the priest he was given wisdom, not knowledge, and that was much better. He also cultivated his imagination with garbage sorting.

Ram in this metropolis slum, without really knowing it, was given wisdom that had been transmitted down all the way from Shakyamuni. Even if it was a life of garbage collection or even if he became a rickshaw puller, or even got a job where he would wear a uniform, this wisdom became the guiding principle in Ram's life.

Amongst those people in India who pick up garbage for their whole lives, there are many great philosophers and wise men. It might be because in such a dodgy place as the slum they appear quite haggard looking, or even as simple rickshaw pullers.

Although, the direction of Ram's life was uncertain, he would surely maintain the good faith of his parents and the blessings of the priest as well as upholding the Buddha's teachings. It was his mission of sorts being born as someone from Bihar. He was born amongst the cosmopolitan mix that is New Delhi.

Anyone meeting Ram in twenty or thirty years would certainly be surprised with India shedding the old, just as a pupa turns into a butterfly.

Ram in the slums today, just as any other day quietly sorted trash and picked up dreams.

Just as Gandhi's spinning wheel alluded to the industrial revolution, Ram's job likewise alluded to the civilization of consumerism and warned about environmental destruction.

Ram was certainly a true practitioner of environmentalism That in itself might truly be the modern day practice of Bodhisattvas.

Comment:

There are so many slums in Indian metropolitan cities and most of the foreigners who visit India think it is nothing but misery in such places, but in actuality they are living with joy and happiness. Due to the population density in the urban areas and industrialization of the sub-urban areas, slums still continue to grow. I try to depict the real life in the slums and the people there who actually live quite eco-friendly lifestyles.

Raju's Dreams

In the desert of Rajasthan at a crossroads there was a tea shop where Raju worked. Raju was still ten years old, but the owner was lost in gambling and the actual work of the shop was left to Raju.

Raju's parents were a part of a caravan that crossed the desert with camels carrying goods. Until his parents returned, he was left at the tea shop.

In the modern day, camel caravans had become old fashioned, and as there was tension between India and Pakistan, there were no roads. The borders were guarded, but they were quite long and because they were right in the middle of the desert there were no inclinations by anyone to build a fence. It was forbidden for people to cross, but camels belonged neither to India nor Pakistan and religious affiliations, whether it be Hindu or Muslim, were of no consequence. The camels were overlooked.

Everybody knew there were people riding atop the camels and goods strapped to the sides of the camels, but their existence was something of a fixture in the Rajasthan desert.

That is why when they were some distance away from the border, the people were the masters of the camels, but when they approached the border, the camels became the masters and the humans became mere cargo. The people stopped existing as humans in a sense. They were like the armies written into the constitutions of both countries.

"Believing it does not exist, despite it is existing."

"Believing it does exist, despite it is not existing."

These people had unconsciously adopted some philosophical thoughts into their lives and lived a life free of any doubts.

58

It was in such an environment that Raju worked in a tea shop. Raju's job was to give water and take orders whenever customers came in. The water was drawn from a well. You had to use a lot of energy to pump it out. Whenever the owner was lost in some conversation with somebody, he would make himself some sweet milk tea.

Truth be told, people did not really come here to drink tea, rather to just spend some time chatting with the owner.

The local people did not read newspapers. They came to the shop to exchange information. While listening to the adults discuss things; he would become a truck driver, a farmer, a merchant and sometimes a construction worker. It was like a magical ability to make oneself somebody else. He would enter the minds of others and while he worked rather hard his mind was as free as a bird.

Raju's joy was having his parents return home and being able to see them when the camel caravan returned. Even when his parents did not return for some time they would send him care packages. His parents were in an underground circle, so they never spoke to him of work. Still the camels provided stories about the desert. The stories about camels that customers would tell was a great learning experience even though Raju didn't attend school.

59

Some of Raju's ancestors had been the poorest in this desert region of Rajasthan, but over two hundred years prior they had abandoned it for a time and wrapped in a single blanket of wool, they rode their camels into central India. During the time of the British Empire, they wandered from town to town trading. In one town, they might have a lot of something and in another village they might have a shortage of it. They eventually became quite wealthy.

Not only that, they spread their wings to the horizon and went to places like Europe, America and Africa. They became caravans without camels.

Many of the wealthy people in India were called Marwaris and they were these desert people. However, those who never left Rajasthan continued running their caravans with camels.

Ironically, those people in the Ganges river areas live on the most fertile soils. Even without spreading fertilizer on their land they can grow things. They are quite fortunate, but they need only pray to God and have no need to really use their heads much, so in modern India the people on the most fertile lands are quite poor and the desert people, originally from barren lands, have conquered the Indian economy.

Indeed, when people have driven up the wall, they hang on for a dear life.

Indeed, when people don't have a penny to their name, they get the will to do something.

One day an old man with a cane in his hand came for tea, wearing a pure white garment. He grinned listening to the chatter of everyone and kept a close eye on Raju going about his work.

In the teachings of Hinduism, the elderly often take a final journey at the end of their lives. They throw away everything and wander until their life comes to an end.

The old man when he was Raju's age abandoned the desert and crossed the ocean to England. He started off as a shoe-shine boy and then eventually owned a shop before starting to trade. He became so wealthy that he didn't really know how much he had, but at the end of his life, he wanted to see his home where was he born and in such simple attire he happened to visit the tea shop.

Having directly faced his own death and already satisfied with his success in life, he merely wanted to be enveloped in the old sands of his hometown rather than returning triumphantly to demonstrate his success to everyone else.

You cannot bring to the heavens above your wealth, land, reputation, success or anything else. The old man thought perhaps his life until then had just been a mirage, so he left England and returned to India. He then met Raju, a young man with glittering eyes.

Raju knew nothing of the old man's past. He somehow felt that the old man's stories were different from the usual stories the adults told in the tea shop – they were closer to the stories about camels. He thought perhaps he had indeed found somebody to talk to whom he could sympathize with. The old man and Raju became friends.

Truth be told Raju was alone. He really couldn't speak of anything but camels.

The old man was likewise alone. He had too much wealth and all the issues connected with passing it down to his children had caused a stir in his family. There was also the issue of the company heir. That's why until now he couldn't open his mouth to anyone but lawyers.

Camels and lawyers are quite different, but the camels carry heavy cargo and the lawyers help with carrying life's burdens. Just looking superficially at the two they were different, but for Raju and the old man they were the same animal.

The old man and Raju did indeed become friends.

When the old man was Raju's age, he crossed the ocean to England and was shining shoes at Victoria Station. He would look up at the customers from down below and then cast his gaze down as he went to work shining the shoes. Though he looked up to people, in his later years he was never looked down upon by others, but rather he came to be respected.

England had controlled India, so it allowed this old man to buy land in London and become a real-estate tycoon.

In his short life, his lifestyle had gone from one extreme to another. His roots in the earth had been uprooted and become mere flowers – pretty, but lacking substance and utility. That's why he felt the need to search out his roots again and happened to meet Raju.

The tea shop's owner, who was quite fond of gambling, always said, "Some day, one day, I'll definitely get rich!" It was a world of delusion that he lived in.

But now Raju had met this old man who was saying, "I've been there and done that." It was like a melody being sung solo from his heart. In his heart was great satisfaction and just a wee bit of space leftover.

The tea shop owner's eyes glistened. The old man smelled of old grass.

As Raju spoke to the old man he somehow felt that a change had occurred in his heart. The old man felt the same. The old man and Raju were life friends who shared the same heart. In any time of life for either of them it would have been the same feeling. They just hadn't had the opportunity to experience it until now.

The old man asked Raju, "Raju, what is your dream?"

Raju replied, "Well, I'd like to go somewhere far away. I want to fly through the sky and cross the ocean. I want to go somewhere so far away that not even the camels could go there."

Raju then posed a question, "Sir, please tell me your dream!"

The old man replied, "Yes, yes ... I used to think, 'I want to go somewhere far away. To fly through the sky and cross the ocean. To go somewhere so far away that not even the camels can go there. But then in my old age I thought, 'I want to return!' So I came here. And, my dream now is to have a dream. That's why I was blown by the wind and ended up back here."

The old man then posed a question. "Raju, what is the happiest thing in life?"

Raju said, "When my mother and father return home riding camels with souvenirs!"

Raju then asked, "Sir, what has been the best thing so far in your life?"

"It was the greatest moment that my dream was no longer just a dream. When your dream is no longer a dream, it isn't a dream! So, maybe, when I had a dream... that was really the greatest. It would have been better had I understood this earlier, but maybe the detours as a result of not understanding was fun. You can live well even with nothing at all provided you have your heart."

Raju felt reassured. He was living and had a heart. He was convinced that as long as he had the dream of crossing the ocean and flying through the sky to go to some faraway place, it would be the greatest dream to have.

The old man looked at Raju warmly and felt pacified. Because whenever he spoke with his children and grandchildren about the future it was always about inheritance, company rights and other arguments. When he compared his own children, who never worked a day in their lives, to Raju, he could only sigh.

Raju looked at the old man and was comforted. He was worked hard by the dodgy tea shop owner and truck drivers and though nobody ever treated him well in the past, the old man was now kind to him and his longing for his parents somewhat lessened. Still, the old man was a traveller and Raju knew it.

It was a hangout for drifters. The people you met today would no longer be here tomorrow. You also had no idea where they went. Like the footsteps in the sands of a desert, the wind blows just a bit and they vanish. Raju sighed.

The two were calmed by each other yet sighed together. The old man and Raju were now close friends.

The old man was confident that his spiritual inheritance would be passed down through Raju and not his children or grandchildren. It was the wisdom of the desert people. It was something that his children, who had been born and raised in prosperous England, could not understand. He made himself understand that even if he had tried to explain to them it would have been impossible.

"Clear your ears and listen to the tidings of the wind. Listen to the counsel of the wind and ride the wind." Such a message he could not convey to them.

It was like trying to trace a path in the desert. You can make your own path, but trying to trace your footsteps is impossible as the wind blows and they vanish. You cannot cling to the paths of the past.

The desert wisdom of clearing one's ears for the tidings of the wind was something he had unconsciously retained even in his metropolis lifestyle.

The old man would now come everyday to drink tea and Raju would speak to him. The old man was quite delighted to treat the townsfolk to tea. The dodgy owner felt a bit more energetic as well owing to this generous customer. He still didn't know who the old man was or even what kind of character he was.

Indeed, perhaps that was for the better because if the tea shop owner came to know who he was, he might become even greedier and that would make it difficult for the old man to stay. For recollecting old times one needed the bottom of a big tree, and perhaps this place was a hindrance.

People from the mere smallest catalyst can have their path in life opened up.

This old man in his youth would shine shoes everyday at Victoria Station. He once came to know an old man, who left him a tip and became the man's errand boy where he was taught trading. He became a clerk and then slowly became independent.

People are not successful just by chance. In the case of this old man, he had a glitter of a dream in his eyes and rode that wave across the sea and society. The final place he arrived at was here in the desert where he was born.

The old man had cleared his ears well and listened to the wind of the desert. Raju was now likewise doing the same with him.

The old man had returned to his hometown and had found a successor to receive his spiritual inheritance. He didn't need a lawyer or a legal will for this. Raju did not attend school, but he had stumbled upon a teacher of life. The old man's wisdom passed through the spirit and was conveyed onto Raju.

It was the whispers of the desert wind and the brilliant twinkling of stars in a clear night sky.

Raju would certainly just like the old man cross the mountain and pass over mountains and ascend to the peaks of human existence.

Then when his life was coming to an end he would doze off into the whispers of the winds of the Rajasthan desert where camels live and recollect the dreams he had actualized in life. Again, he would find a youth just like he once was and have a dialogue about the soul.

Finally, one day the old man was about to slip into the winds and vanish into the desert. He handed Raju a key tucked into a key holder with a four digit number inscribed on it. He said his last words to Raju:

"When you cross the ocean, you will understand."

Comment:

In India children work very hard. Most of the state of Rajasthan is desert. However, one of the tribes called Marwari left Rajasthan and became the richest community in India. They are present not only within India, but overseas as well. This story is about a poor boy in Rajasthan and a Marwari gentleman living in London.

The Last Days of Jizō in Japan

A grime covered Jizō statue, seemingly long forgotten, stood at the corner of a road leaning slightly forward. For a long time he had been forgotten by the townspeople and overlooking a thoroughfare of busy traffic he watched the passage of time. Jizō is known as the Bodhisattva Kṣitigarbha in India. In Japan he often appears as a bald monk holding a staff.

When people had gone to sleep and the traffic ceased for at least a little while, one could hear the voice of this Jizō statue speaking to himself. The surveying for street expansion work had begun.

The first to notice was an old stray cat named Tama. Now the local dogs and birds all knew about it, too. They lent their ears to Jizō, but unfortunately humans were all too busy with their lives, so they lacked the ears to really hear Jizō. Still, I think I can tell you all about Jizō's quiet whispers.

Jizō, very much loves children and so often stands close to playgrounds.

When the streets are quiet, if you listen carefully with the stray cat Tama, you might hear some whispers if you're still a child. Adults might laugh at you, but then they have lost the ability to hear these whispers.

"Long long ago I came from the distant land in India together with Shakayamuni Buddha. We came with Avalokiteśvara and Mañjuśrī."

"I didn't like being held behind by everyone else, so I left the temple and wandered the villages. I came to a place where children played and decided I should always protect them."

"I love children very much, but it is hard to have children come into the temple and allow them to play there, which is entirely absurd."

"My companion Mañjuśrī was in charge of education. Avalokiteśvara, also known as Kannon in Japan and Guanyin in China, was in charge of compassion. Bhaiṣajyarāja, otherwise known as Medicine King Bodhisattva, was in charge of medicine and healing. We divided the jobs of Shakyamuni Buddha and spread out across Japan."

"Though I don't really know the reasons,

Avalokiteśvara was well decorated and got to stand inside big temples and on top of big mountains with everyone folding their hands to him. Mañjuśrī, Samantabhadra and Bhaiṣajyarāja likewise all got to live in temples. Ācala seemingly always angry, was a retainer like me, got a promotion and now stands proudly under a roof."

"I am the only one who has to stand out on a street corner in the rain. Although, I am already a good old age, they put a red bib on me and on top of that despite living a single life and having never married, people give me the responsibility of looking after aborted children who were never born and are said to 'return' to wherever they came from."

"Shakyamuni and Bodhisattvas usually don't ever have traffic accidents, but my kind are run over by cars, they are decapitated, their legs are severed and suffer the expansion of lanes on roads and new city zoning – my kind, really suffer religious persecution! They are exiled from places, tossed away, placed and forgotten beside graves, and sometimes for long periods they have to be around incense smoke, so their health isn't so good."

"It isn't that I am jealous or anything, but one has to wonder why humans do this kind of discrimination and ill-treatment? I'm separated from temples and though I came here to look after the children and be with them, the playground of children has become their rooms and the classroom, so my reason for existence is long since gone."

"I often think of going back to India, but recently I hear the cries of children and worry too much about them, so I cannot go back."

"In old days, children from a young age were made to work. They were separated from their parents and apprenticed in various trades. I would give them some solace, but compulsory education came around and everyone went to school. They didn't have to work anymore and didn't have to worry about that anymore."

"But then before you knew it, the duty of the government to give children an education became a duty of the children to go to school. Before long, their eyes looked empty and vacant."

"I think you need to change the name of compulsory education to conscript education or forced education."

"The kids in the old days who became apprenticed and worked still had more light in their eyes!"

"I have an affinity for kids, so all kids – those who don't go to school, those who are violent, those who bully, those who are bullied – I think they are all cute and I love them all."

"Children are a mirror of society – the prophets of tomorrow. When the environment is destroyed, the kids' playgrounds get affected and there are no more children who come to me."

"Though I try to protect kids, I really can't. People are really mistaken – they stick a bib around my neck and ask me to look after the souls of aborted babies. So, I'm busy looking after them and don't have enough time to look after the living kids."

The stray cat Tama, just nodded its head.

Jizō's best friend used to be a stray black cat named

Kuro, but one day he was caught trespassing in the hospital and sent to the gas chamber.

There used to be just one person who would visit Jizō everyday and make offerings of flowers and food. She was a granny from the neighbourhood. One day her son showed up and took her away to a lonely old folk's home far far away.

Soon a new lane on the road would be built and this Jizō statue would be hauled off and dumped into some desolate cemetery. Thinking about how there would no longer be anyone here to look after the children would be enough to make you cry.

"Most of my companions have returned to India. I have nobody to speak to anymore. I am exhausted, Tama, and perhaps should just return to India and seclude myself in the Himalayas."

"Farewell."

"Trying to convince people to love the children that I look after rather than making the roads bigger to accommodate cars that belch out poisonous fumes is simply impossible."

"Farewell, Tama."

As Jizō said that he really did become stone.

All the Jizōs in all the towns across Japan are going back to India.

Tomorrow, if you find a Jizō statue nearby, you should ask if this Jizō now will really protect us or if he has turned to stone and returned to India.

If you should offer flowers and food and the Jizō cracks a smile, then you know he is protecting you. If he is just as stiff as a rock then Jizō's spirit should be in the mountains of the Himalayas looking after his body which has probably already been damaged by pollution.

But there is nothing to worry about. If you seek out Jizō's aid then he would descend from the Himalayas like a migratory bird and help you.

So, by all means say to the stone Jizō, "Good morning! Good afternoon! Good night!"

Though a stone Jizō, he surely believes in you more than adults or your teachers who can never be reasoned with. Even for children who have done terrible things, he is still far better than adults who start wars or destroy Jizō statues. Jizō will turn to stone if one of those adults who play innocent, shows up asking for favours. However, for kids like you, he will become, the friendly Jizō.

You will all certainly be able to find a Jizō statue somewhere in your neighbourhood.

Comment:

This story concerns the education system in Japan. Negative aspects have arisen due to modernization and tradition, culture and faith have been largely destroyed. Buddhism has a belief in Bodhisattvas. Bodhisattvas have their own promise to liberate sentient beings and this story mentions such a Bodhisattva practice.

The Pilgrim Monk

There was once a monk on a pilgrimage who wandered from village to village.

In old days there were multitudes of them, but now they have become really few and one has almost no chance of meeting a monk walking through villages with his begging bowl.

This monk, living in today's society, walked, took the train, rode in the cars of the people he met, sometimes, took a plane and went to various countries. If somebody asked him to recite a *sūtra*, he would recite it. If someone wanted to talk, he would talk with them. If someone had some worry on their mind, he would listen. He made pilgrimages to any and all places at whim.

One day he went to visit a temple atop a mountain he had not been to and relaxing there by himself in the forest, a small bird came fluttering down and perched on his shoulder. It was a cute little parakeet with a red beak and green feet.

The monk said to himself, "Well, did you fly away from someone's cage only to become a lost bird, I wonder?" He raised a hand to his shoulder and the bird jumped onto his hand and chirped in his ear. From thereon the monk and the little bird became friends wandering from town to town.

Though, he met many people and had many discussions on a myriad of topics, at the end of the day people would return home and the lone monk would alone retire to some room in a temple, inn or some friend's spare room. He would tend to himself and rest.

The little bird would always go away strangely somewhere, but sometimes in the evening when the monk was lying down and resting, it would come unannounced and perch on the monk's shoulder chirping away.

More strangely was that listening to the chirping of the bird he would doze off and have a dream.

The dreams were like a recollection of some long past thing or even a revelation of sorts. Some were sweet, others bitter and some were pleasurable, others were sad. They would start with the chirping of the bird and he would awaken from the dream when the bird flew away. After training for so long, he thought perhaps these dreams might actually make a reality out of his longing, as it were, to grow wings and fly away from the world of suffering.

Unfortunately, he had no wings. The little bird perched on his shoulder chirping and the dreams it summoned was the only way he was able to fly.

He never knew where the little bird would fly off to, but he would always return with the dust of the world on his wings.

The monk had for a long time wandered around at whim, visiting many places and as a result knew many people and places, but he disliked the dust of the world and avoided it living a life where he tried to never even gaze upon it.

However, this dust that the little bird brought with it was different from what he had been thinking it was, until now. It was a mix of happiness, sorrow and pain. It was bitter, but a good and effective medicine.

If he happened to inhale the dust or put his face near the wings of the bird he had now quite disliked it. It was something he found disagreeable – to be rejected, and thought of as no good and nothing more than that. However, that preconception faded and moulded together with his dream.

His preconceptions were not made from ideas or even beliefs, but something that gushed from the depths of his spirit, though it was sublime and seemed like a belief or idea – it sounded as if it had been a message from the Buddha, but was it really?

When he tried to think about it a moment and whisper to the little bird, it jumped and flew away.

Humans can do nothing but walk. One might use the advances of technology, but there is still a limited degree to which a human can fly – one cannot freely fly at whim like a bird.

The monk realized that he had been mistaken until now seeking wings in his heart to fly – moving from place to place on many pilgrimages, meeting many people and making giant leaps.

He strangely wanted to say this to the little bird, but though he waited and waited, the little bird did not return.

Certainly, the little bird had been sent from above to convey the realization to the monk of his slanted view of the world and his lonely heart.

In this great open sky, there is no system, frame or rules, and one uses wings to fly freely. In order to have the monk realize his own fabricated world was ultimately a product of his own ideas, he sung to him in a beautiful voice and conveyed this message in his dreams.

From the day the little bird left, the monk realized he was just a single person and nothing special – he felt stupid, ugly, disagreeable, intrusive and full of himself. Though people may fold their hands to him, he had no qualifications to really speak to people. With shame and a face showing signs of humiliation he felt not even like a person, but just an organism.

At that moment, the little bird suddenly appeared. The little parakeet had golden feathers and was a phoenix flying towards the sun.

As the bird fluttered, a single golden feather fell from the sky.

The monk thought this would be a useful good luck charm for his pilgrimage, picked up the golden feather and placed his chest pocket – the wings of the heart he had been seeking for so long now took root in his spirit.

He was no longer living a life based on the idea of doing a job – the job of a pilgrim monk who wears a robe and shaves his head, lives just like an organism. He was no longer a monk bound by preconceptions and predetermined rules, but had obtained golden wings in his heart and could fly freely.

The monk was not able to live without caring what worldly people said or how they understood him – he now had wings of the heart and was able to become a truly universal being embracing everyone and everything.

If you ever see a monk travelling from town to town, be sure to see if he has golden wings in his heart. Those who have the wings are called a monk. Those without those wings are just doing the job of a monk.

Comment:

Nowadays, most of the clergy are living in churches or temples and working within their own individual frameworks. In particular, after the industrial revolution, people have been brain-washed into choosing just one profession or speciality. However, human beings have every aspect and potential within them. This story tries to explain the potentiality of the human being through the example of a wandering monk.

Annie's Middle Way

Annie was born in Stuttgart in the south of Germany. When she was young her parents got divorced and she lived with her father and elder brother.

When Annie was in junior high school she began to wonder whether or not she had been born in the wrong country. So when she was eighteen years old she at last came to India. While visiting various holy places, she came to know a Tibetan family in the Himalayan Mountains and she became a Buddhist.

In that village she received a Tibetan name "Dechen" from a monk. Appearance wise she was German, but in her heart she was Tibetan Dechen.

There was something about her that was different from other Tibetan girls of the same age. It was that she came to always wonder if she had been mistakenly born a girl. The more she spent time thinking about it, she started feeling a bit odd. However, she reached the age of twenty and a beautiful feminine glow came from within. As much as possible she wore old clothes and hung a *mala* around her neck. She always walked with a humble downcast gaze.

Girls of her same age tried to dress to look beautiful. However, Annie, who had already obtained beauty, disliked this and completely rejected it. That was because in the middle way, which is beautifying the mind, you keep in mind the principle that the surface appearances will inevitably become shabby looking.

Annie was a foreigner so every six months she had to return to Germany. She would then make some money and again go to practice and meditate in the Himalayan Mountains.

At a young age her mother had abandoned her. This was becoming a great force in rejecting the woman within her.

Having been born in Germany, a disciplined and an almost automated nation, the idea of moving to free-spirited India triggered her spirit.

"Annie" and "Dechen" lived in the same heart, but became two personalities. Sometimes they mingled and sometimes they resisted and became isolated from each other.

It was there that someone from a completely different far eastern country got right in the middle of Annie and Dechen. He could talk to Annie and could also talk to Dechen. It was because he had come from Japan, an odd contradiction filled country mixed with western and eastern civilizations as well as Buddhist traditions.

At the time when it felt like her spirit was about to fracture she rode the eastern winds at the Buddha's grace and good fortunes came.

Now, Annie and Dechen went with the winds from the east. In order to pull together her mind she secluded herself in a cave. It was because she needed time to put together two personalities.

Then, after doing just that a person who was neither a westerner nor an easterner, could pass through anywhere in the world, was reborn.

Her wounds from childhood had been healed, and now she would go to help others.

Until then she had been Annie, Dechen, a practitioner of meditation, a woman – six months in Germany, six months in India; a western body and an eastern heart. She had to live inside a cave in-between her western traits and a longing for the east.

The world has become small and we are now able to freely travel around. The interaction between people is also flourishing. Annie's "contradiction of the heart" more or less applies to everyone in the world.

Those people who cannot stand this, end up in fundamentalist movements where their minds are seemingly stuck in the past with a time machine, and only their bodies are left to antagonize others. Being able to gently deal with the modern mixed world is a teaching of tolerance – it is the light of the Buddha's compassion.

We don't pray to become "chosen people", but that all living things can become Buddhas. Annie's journey of the heart is a pointer for the world's people and their own journeys with the "contradictions of the heart".

Comment:

Annie is a real story about a girl who stayed at my temple and practiced Buddhism. When her visa expired, she would return to Germany. She was quite young and pure, but she struggled between western civilization and eastern philosophy. This story is applicable to many western visitors arriving in India when they start to practice Buddhism or Hinduism.

Baba and the Dropouts

In India the word *bakushīshi* means, "How blessed!" *"Baba"* doesn't mean Papa. You call a monk or priest *Baba*.

Nobody knows *Baba's* past. No matter how much you questioned him, he would just reply with a vague response about his past, and fail to reveal any real details, so everyone had lost interest.

Just by being able to speak English, scribble on paper some incomprehensible letters and utter strange things, the local shop keepers all took a backseat to his abilities.

Baba was always of a humble character, but for some reason whenever you wanted to receive a blessing he held his head up high chanting, "*bakushīshi, bakushīshi, bakushīshi* ..." while ringing his bell.

Baba gathered merit through offering blessings and letting others know he was offering them that chance without saying it outright.

You might think of that as some kind of selfishness, but he was actually the pride of India's poorest people and even a guide for the religious.

Wealth is a matter of chance. Before you know it flows away from you. Water too becomes rain from a cloud and flows into the river, eventually into the sea and then becomes a cloud again only to moisten the Himalaya Mountains.

Baba in his long years of life experience and his work, where he had poured blessings down from the high to the low, was just a natural working of nature.

Most of the time he just sat humbly by the roadside and gazed at people from below. However, when a blessing was bestowed on someone, a certain dignity had to be maintained in order to properly transfer the merit. He had to hold his chin up high because the verses were bestowed in God's name.

Unfortunately, nobody could comprehend that "internal world" of his and so he was just a strange beggar monk to most people in New Delhi station.

It was there when *Baba* made friends with some youth known as "dropouts" who hailed from those mistakenly self-declared "developed nations". These countries thought of themselves as better developed so those who did not think so and those who noticed that mistake, fell straight down from the rooftops of buildings and became a tribe of "dropouts".

In front of the station there was a poor street. The ordinary city residents of New Delhi did not go there. They absolutely despised it. However, India is not really a country of "city residents".

Is it the public or humankind? For the people who lived not hiding the true essence of humanity, it was an oasis where one spent the night in the big city.

This tribe of "dropouts", like a room of mirrors in a fairy tale, had knowledge of the opposite side of the real world. How much money you have and how dirty an appearance you sported was an object of respect.

In the real world, a person being rich and having a clean appearance or a person up-to-date on the latest news and gossip is respected, but here it was the opposite. He, who wandered across India for how many years wearing tattered garments and having neither spare change nor cash on hand – not knowing at all what was going on in the outside world – was an object of respect.

He, who had just arrived with plenty of cash in his pocket and presented the image of a sparkling clean traveller found himself hesitant in front of these people.

When you fall down head over heels, the basis of your values goes head first.

Here titles didn't apply. The shock of the first impression is what determined the hierarchy. They were truly a tribe of the jungle that is the city.

Like drummers of ancient times, this tribe of "dropouts" also enjoyed festivals. Everyday you would add new friends to the circle and eat, drink and be merry. Then you would start meditation with everyone.

Everyone believed in a kind of strange book – it was a thick guidebook not unlike a holy book or a desktop reference. It was a religious text that taught how to travel as cheaply as possible and applied that thinking to all the worldly matters and affairs. This was the bible for the "dropout" tribe. A guidebook is actually just something you use as a reference, but for these people believing in it was their behavioural principle.

It was there that *Bakushīshi Baba* appeared. A single lone youth came to India searching for something.

What it was that he sought after he really didn't know – you might place it as mental disease under the "doesn't know anything" disease category.

When a person becomes sick their sensitivities become sharper. So, while other youth quickly became "dropouts", he was, simply put, unable to change his principles within modern society. At that time he met *Baba*.

Baba, the beggar then came to have a disciple. There is an old proverb of monks begging for three days without quitting. That youth successfully cleared those three days and became a beggar.

The severity of living with people's pity, the cozy comfort of devoting oneself to blessing others and the ego that was within oneself till then all melted away like ice cream in the scorching Indian sun.

He emulated *Baba's* calm step and always trailed behind him. The people on the street at first roared with laughter, but as it became part of the everyday scene, people would come to look forward to seeing *Baba* and the youth.

People for the longest time continued to have a distorted perception of the foreigners. Even though they sported dirty appearances, the people all had this irritating feeling of wanting to make fun of them but not being able to – those young people on their accord had come from countries, rode on planes and held passports all of which were unavailable to the regular people there.

With the arrival of the youth, he gained a chance to be blessed. In the act of blessing, there has to be a feeling of compassion. If you don't think, "How pitiful!" then you don't give food or change.

The people on the street came to have a better opinion of *Baba*. The shop owners got money from the foreign youth. *Baba* had captured the heart of a foreign youth and made him a disciple. The truth is that *Baba* was a saint. People came to New Delhi and surrounded him. *Baba* became the respected head of the "dropouts".

Even today here around New Delhi that old bell rings and *Baba* while chanting "*bakushīshi, bakushīshi, bakushīshi ...*" goes around storefronts. The youths also follow. India has received a lot of aid from foreign countries and developed greatly, but here the people still make their offerings. The value of money is different, but the people will repay kindness.

Consoling the wounded youth who had fallen from the rooftops of developed countries and blessing them with a meal and some tea is how modern India repays kindness. Bakushīshi *Baba* was the spiritual leader.

If you come to India you'll definitely be able to meet Bakushīshi *Baba*. When you do please follow him. At first it might be embarrassing, but if you can tough it out for three days, you'll be wholly absorbed into it. You'll also know the depth of India's bosom. Your stomach will also be full. Also, please take it easy and have an afternoon nap while you're at it.

Then you should heal your wounds and again scale up the tall building. Your father, mother and friends are all waiting for you.

Comment:

This story compares developing nations and developed nations. In ancient times as it is now, those who are a little crazy yet speak wisdom, are considered holy in some places. In India such people became *sadhus*. This story explains how ordinary people treat such *sadhus* and how *sadhus* live and behave. Backpackers are often impressed by such a lifestyle.

Kuttā – The Dog Saint

In India you call a dog *kuttā*. There was a nameless *kuttā* – a stray dog really – in Varanasi. He was a mere scrawny bag of bones. From the day he could open his eyes this stray *kuttā* saw the hustle and bustle of the holy city of Varanasi. His mother too had been a stray.

In this part of India, the idea of raising a dog as a pet was unheard of. Some very wealthy people would occasionally buy a guard dog, but you seldom saw them on the street. You could just hear them growling on the other side of the wall. For them, human society was like a prison where they were chained, their freedom taken away and then they were confined within walls.

So, the stray dogs of India, no matter how skinny they became, never had in the slightest a feeling of envy towards those guard dogs with a roof over their heads.

Maybe rather than being a "stray dog" they were "wild dogs" or maybe even "free dogs" and like horses, sheep, cows and people they had the relative freedom to roam the streets. Unfortunately, dogs and people both had almost no conception of human rights let alone dog rights, so *kuttā* was simply just a stray dog in the eyes of most people.

Kuttā really loved the poor people. The rich folks however would drive their cars and make everyone, including people and dogs, get out of the way. They also had no thought of feeding either dog or man.

The poor people had no refrigerators, so they tossed away their leftover food and rice. Perhaps it was bad manners, but in the cheap eateries on the side of streets under the tables they would discard bones from their meals as well as burnt pieces of chapati that nobody wanted to eat. Sometimes, the boy hauling water would boot them out, but then the dogs would lower their tails and whine a bit and the boy would pretend not to see them.

But you know dogs all have their own territories. A stray dog might not really be a pet dog, but he knows he is a kind of pet to people in a certain area and he makes a point of letting the other dogs know it. However, they don't need to maintain their territory just on strength alone. As long as there were kids who paid them a bit of attention or old folks with a bit of pity for them, the dogs were looked after.

Self-defence in dog society as well as a balance of diplomacy in human society both preserve lives.

The holy city of Varanasi is the heart and soul of India. It is a refuge for the heart. This also applies to animals. In those streets both people and animals together form a kind of symbiotic life.

Kuttā was well aware he was a stray dog in a holy city. Day after day at the side of the Ganges River he saw bodies being cremated before his very eyes and he could also smell it. A dog's sense of smell is a thousand times more than a human's. *Kuttā* was able to know various things unknowable to humans because of his nose. However, he knew no way of transmitting that knowledge to people and perhaps that was for the best.

Today, *Kuttā* was out sniffing around for food and while having a pee at the side of the road he thought of the ways of people and dogs.

Do you know what kind of self-awareness a dog has? A human cannot really understand it. It's a realization of smell. A dog has a sense of smell a thousand times stronger than that of a human, so humans cannot comprehend it. Humans have far too much confidence in their own abilities. They don't believe or see the abilities that animals have.

It's really just the police that have the sense to call on the help of a dog in an investigation.

Kuttā's realization of smell was the ability to smell the scent of a soul and know the length of someone's life.

Everyday in Varanasi people were born and died. The bodies were set ablaze at the side of the Ganges and sent floating downstream. The stream of life flowed like that of the Ganges and *Kuttā* could actually sense this as a scent.

Everyone entrusted the bones of their deceased loved ones to the Ganges. In *Kuttā*'s heart there was a kind of golden flowing spirit of a river that was like the Ganges. When he went to the riverbank, the water there had a smell. When he stood in the stream he could smell the echoes of the spirits in the water. *Kuttā* understood this was the realization of smell. Though his life was short he was quite happy to have been born here.

All the beings in Varanasi do not fear death as they look at the river of spirits and entrust their body and mind to the river. That's why those gruesome cremation pyres are surrounded not by fear and loathing but rather by a soft and friendly atmosphere.

Today, like any other day, *Kuttā* was whining at the side of a bustling street looking for food. He was also sniffing out and following the footsteps of his predecessors in preparing to return to that river of spirits.

Kuttā was something of an ascetic dog. If you ever visit Varanasi you'll most certainly meet him.

Comment:

This story illustrates the potential of a dog. Usually, human beings always think that humanity is the supreme species on the planet. However, many animals possess superior senses. So, we should avoid looking down on animals as they actually know things that we do not.

Following the Wind

Tomo-chan wasn't her real name. Anytime and anywhere she could make friends, so people called her Tomo-chan which means little friend.

Here you would call a kid who became friends with a particular group as *dachi*. Then, you would call the kids who sat on the side of the road, at the station or in the park as *dachiko*.

It was really good that Tomo-chan was never called *dachi*.

Tomo-chan just loved flying around like the wind. Even though she didn't do things like the other girls, she remained unconcerned about such things.

That's why she didn't wear makeup. She also didn't like pretty clothes. She also absolutely despised household chores. However, because she had a big heart she went to all the restaurants and eateries on the street and thought of them as her own kitchen and knew everything about them. Thus, she was a kind of walking dictionary and encyclopaedia on matters related to eating cheap and delicious food. Indeed, she was a B-class gourmet kind of a girl.

However, whether she was A, B or C it didn't matter as long as she got to be called a queen. Then, she was completely satisfied. Now, she might lose to the ace of spades and the king of hearts, but with time and age she would see a complete reversal, become grandma and maybe rule the world.

Still, having the image of "grandma" until your later years would have you lose out on life, so now that was a kind of big life problem for her. But because she had a big heart, she thought of the whole world as her own backyard. Also, she thought of all the kids she met as her own children. This is why nobody could ever comprehend her. They all thought she was a weirdo. People all make their own stereotypes and they're set in stone. They're heavy and don't ever fly anywhere.

Tomo-chan was different. In order to preserve Tomo-chan she had to become like the wind and fly. That's why people could feel her without having anything to grasp, just like the wind.

The truth is if your heart becomes big, so does your body – this is really a common knowledge. If your heart becomes too big, you'll become like an elephant! They say those with small little hearts all become little people.

But then the vastness of the body and the depth of the heart do not always seem in proportion. Tomo-chan was prone to be stick thin. That's why nobody could imagine her big heart.

Today she was riding her bike around the street sniffing out the wind. Tomo-chan was stick thin, but she was cute She had a mobile phone strung to her neck as a decoration. Such things tie and bind people with radio waves.

But Tomo-chan was still quite composed and calm. When she experienced the truth in life that both her mom and dad could not clutch the wind in their hands it was a sure sign she had become an adult.

She thought it was necessary to know the direction of the wind as a kind of indicator in life, so she carried the mobile phone.

Tomo-chan one day at long last had become friends with the wind.

If she was ever to be called *dachi* it would be all worry and she'd not even be able to move, so she tried as much as possible never to make friends, but then the wind wasn't human – it was the wind. So, one day she rode and flew with the wind. She passed through the starry skies above and flew around the vast expanse.

It was then that the wind whispered to her, "Where will you go? You can go anywhere! That's because you are the wind." Tomo-chan was so pleased she spun around in circles.

It was then she recalled that all the names of typhoons were named after girls. She learned that at school.

She then replied to the wind saying, "Let's go to the further reaches of the earth! Let's go!"

The wind doesn't know things like a ball being round, but knew things all through experience.

That's because no matter how sad and bad things got, no matter how the tears came down like rain, and no matter how far away to the horizon, it always returned to the same place. It always went back to the start.

That's also why the wind's name became Start and it was happy. When it did poorly, it still, nevertheless returned to the start.

The start of wind was not a mundane knowledge learned at school. It was in risking one's life to know that the earth was round.

Here, it met Tomo-chan in Japan. The wind had tossed away all awful thoughts and decided to go halfway across the world to South America.

That was the farthest place on the planet – it would go to the ends of the earth and return to the original place from whence it came. Tomo-chan burst and ran around like a typhoon.

Over there was a place called the Incan Empire. The civilization of the Incas had flourished, but one day westerners looking for India, crossed the sea and ended up in South America. They had risked their lives looking for spices across the sea, but they somehow ended up on the opposite side of the planet on another continent.

That's life sometimes – you risk your life believing something and it ends up being the exact opposite.

You yourself might laugh at this, but these people changed history the whole 360 degrees. They had thought the opposite side of the planet was India and they even started to think the people in South America were Indians. They even called them Indians!

They then massacred people who had been living peacefully and took away all their gold, silver and precious gems. And so their civilization regressed and nothing but ruins remained.

These people were able to foretell the future. They were actually well aware that westerners would come. They didn't take it as a warning and just accepted it as a prophecy which they believed was set in stone.

The prophecy was actually a warning. They should have taken this prophecy as a warning for themselves, but they believed it was a prophecy which foretold things that were unavoidable.

Tomo-chan ran with the wind and circled the whole of South America. These people spoke to the stars and had a star calendar which nobody could read anymore. It is just believed to be a holy relic.

Tomo-chan for a moment thought she had been bestowed by these people. Here, she thought neighbourhood restaurants were her kitchen at the park which was her own backyard, but then these people had the whole universe as their backyard and house.

Just like Tomo-chan, these people were thought of as odd. Indeed, they were the first people living together with the universe rather against it. That's why the westerners thought they were strange.

The wind then wanted to go to India.

People often longed for India – they risked their lives crossing the sea to this mysterious country. When they learned that India was on the opposite side of the world from South America, their heads spun. The opposite side of the planet was supposed to have been Japan.

Closing their eyes for a minute they became like the wind and circled the planet realizing it isn't a round flat surface, but a sphere with three dimensional lining.

Tomo-chan whispered to the wind.

"Let's become like the Himalayan winds where the Gods live. Let's pick up the clouds and pour down rains. Let's swim in the spirit sea that flows with the Ganges River."

Tomo-chan was delighted. At the limits of the lands she finally arrived at, there was yet another limit to those lands and in the world's tallest mountains she could see the Gods.

She raced past the wind and arrived ahead in India. This little girl was a typhoon. She climbed the Himalayas and with the migrating birds passed all around India.

Those westerners, who had gone looking for spices and risked their lives only to end in the Americas, had made a big mistake. Likewise the English who used magnetic compasses to find India had not found the real India in India.

Looking at it from the outside it looked like Indians were in India, but you entered it and like magic they disappeared! The Indians became Bengalis, Punjabis, Tamils, Tibetans and many other people and then they became Englishmen – the "Indians" suddenly disappeared.

Indeed, India was not a country, but the Indian world or the Indian universe. That's why people longed for it and risked their lives crossing the sea to get to it.

The wind had been held hostage in their sails, but eventually slipped away and arrived in India. The wind became India's wind. The wind of India is a hot wind. It is in the service of the sun. It was heat that roasted any and everything. Touching the ground it summoned a cloud of dust. Still, every year as atonement it gave two months of rain. However, because it was a year's worth of rain it became flood.

Indeed, India went from extreme to extreme.
Dynamite hot curry to sickeningly sweet candy.
Extreme wealth and extreme poverty.
Heat waves and bitter cold.
Colours and colourlessness.
There's no middle in any of it.

In such an extreme world if you don't cry out and assert yourself, you become like a dust cloud and fade away.

The wind called Start and Tomo-chan became the wind of the sun and ran about the entire Indian continent.

The sun everyday rises from the east. It raises its head from beyond the horizon and peaks over. Tomo-chan wanted to go beyond the horizon. She wanted to know where the sun hides itself. So she said to wind named Start, "Let's go beyond the horizon to where the sun hides!" Start knew it – you go beyond the horizon and you end up where you started from. However, that's a wisdom you have to experience and learn. He didn't want to reveal it to Tomo-chan.

It was good just to say "yes, yes" to what the girl said and when they passed over the world, it really was a true feeling that was felt.

At that moment Tomo-chan sneezed. She looked around restlessly and her bike had fallen over. She was in the park. She had dozed off and fallen asleep and slept quite comfortably because the park was her park. She had travelled across the world as the wind in her dreams.

The wind breezed, passed her. It was already evening. The smell from the noodle wagon at the edge of the river was carrying over to where she was.

Her mobile phone then started ringing. Tomo-chan had to make a decision whether to follow the whisper of the wind or her mother's call to dinner. The wind was carrying over the steam from the noodle wagon by the river. Tomo-chan smelled the noodles and made her decision. She went with the wind down towards the river.

Comment:

This story is about how the youngsters in their teenage years between thirteen to seventeen or so develop an inclination towards their spiritual growth.

Kumar – The Travel Guide

In New Delhi there is a travel guide by the name of Kumar who always sits on the side of the streets around the station.

The truth, however, is that though he was a "guide" his actual job was that of a swindler. That was because a lot of foreign travellers would come here for the cheap lodging and tried to travel as cheap as possible and from an Indian common point of view they carried in their pockets a stupid amount of cash.

So, for the first two or three days it might have been expensive, but they listened to what Kumar had to say. What they thought of as a small amount was for an Indian ten times more than normal. That's why he was a swindler.

With a bright smiling face, Kumar would speak in a quite friendly manner and take you all around. He was able to make friends right away just after meeting them for the first time. However, that was limited just to foreigners. If it was an Indian like him and they had met ten times they still would not be friends. Only those who trusted him unconditionally would be his friend and even then it was usually for only a day. That was because if someone became friends with him beyond that, certain things were revealed, attachments would arise and obstacles to his actual vocation would come up.

Kumar's family were poor farmers from the Deccan Plateau. When he had come to Delhi looking for work, a souvenir shop owner took him in.

Really with that kind of seemingly honest face and a sharp personality, he raised sales at the souvenir shop several fold. He then went off on his own and became independent. He became the president of a fictional travel company with just a business card. In reality, he became a sightseeing guide.

His title was that of president, but he would arrange both plane and train tickets and even run errands. Without anyone ever knowing he went along with travellers, swindled and ripped people off. It was a lifestyle of hello and goodbye.

However, he was quite devoted to his parents and always sent home some money. He also sent to his younger siblings an allowance and school fees. He never spoke to his parents about the reality of his job.

For Kumar, it was not an issue of how foreigners would come to view India, either for the better or worse, but about how much money he could send to his poor parents and how much money he could save that was life's real important problem.

When he stopped and thought about what India had done for him and his family till now, he recalled the time when he first arrived in Delhi and also when the cops seemingly had it in for him swindling out of the money. When he went looking for work he also went to the government office where he was treated as a stupid boy from the country. When he thought to vote in the elections his bungled paperwork was met with fingers pointing out errors and in the end he couldn't vote. Even his food subsidy paperwork had yet to be transferred from the countryside to Delhi.

So, when he thought about what India had done for him he came to the conclusion that really it was nothing and so he felt no sense of gratitude at all. He figured that even if he scammed travellers and gave India a bad image it really made no difference to him.

So, Kumar had come from the countryside to Delhi and suffered a wounded heart. He took those wounds as a kind of springboard and by swindling foreigners he showed his disgust. He vowed to himself that he would triumph some day.

He thought it somehow unfair that foreigners younger than him could buy expensive plane tickets and come to India. Moreover, he knew that the salaries in those foreign countries were as much as ten times higher than in India. His idea was that everything could be overcharged tenfold. He wasn't all that good at math, but a simple calculation of tenfold was his standard.

After coming to Delhi he managed to learn a lot about things from word of mouth.

Foreigners also carried travel insurance. If they ever became ill they just went to a top quality hospital and could be admitted without any payment at all. Just a simple phone call overseas and everything was taken care of for them. Even if they lost all their money they had credit cards and traveller's cheques and could get cash right away without any problems. Even if they lost their passport, they just went to the embassy and it was reissued in a single day.

Now, in his case if he became ill he was all alone in the capital city. If he went to a nice clean private hospital a whole month's salary went out the window. If he went to a government hospital it was free, and it was like a field hospital in a war where people are not treated as human. If he lost his money then it was all over. He would have no other choice but to resort to begging. On top of that his parents and siblings in the country would likewise suffer.

He had been going to the government office for close to a year, any number of times for his food subsidy paperwork to be transferred, but it went nowhere.

Those travellers cheated by Kumar were suckers. The truth is those who knew Kumar referred to those travellers as chickens. You had to first consider how to cook them.

Did you make tandoori chicken or chicken curry? Or did you wait until they laid a golden egg? In his youth on the Deccan plateau he had much experience catching animals with nets and decoys and it all came to be quite handy. It was an animal-like instinct. It might have been the blood of his ancestors who used to hunt in the jungle. Then you had to decide whether to quick roast them or stew them, or maybe raise them up on a skillet. There was also a difference between chickens for tandoori and chickens for curry.

So Kumar, day in and day out had to stand in hot weather as hell, outside the station. He would find those foreigners looking a bit dazed and confused and he himself was busy taking care of them. He would take them to hotels as far away as possible. These were the kinds of places that fellow travellers could not speak of. He would then receive some cash from the hotel man and from there show them around the streets.

Those persons who had gotten used to travelling India from the start would not receive his attention. He went for those persons who had come for the first time and were uncertain about things.

The souvenir shops, ear cleaners, rickshaw pullers all worked together with him and charged the foreigners ten times the normal price.

Whenever a traveller started to think something was up he would take them to an acquaintance's house where the father, mother, grandparents, brothers, sisters and relatives would all gather together and eat dinner. Kumar would then pay the household a kind of restaurant fee and as it was a great help to the family, they were all quite receptive and welcoming.

On such a day the whole family would feast, so the kids were quite happy and the guest would relish their attention.

The countries from which the travellers came were all quite affluent and had less of a connection to the family. Seeing an Indian family was quite a shock to them.

So, the traveller would scold themselves for doubting Kumar in the first place and would want to have him as a guide again the next day.

The countries from which these people came were so-called developed nations, but as they sought material progress they came to regard belief in Gods and Buddha as superstitions.

Still, humans have a sense of "belief" nevertheless. These people beyond necessity believed in their system of society, loved ones and themselves. But they still somehow unconsciously felt that contradiction in the back of their minds and set about to visit India.

Here in India people believe in God, but they do not believe in people. They believe in family, but they do not believe in the system of society. They also have arranged marriages, not really believing in themselves. It is always a matter of "us" and not "me".

The travellers would seek in Kumar the "feeling of believing in life". That was Kumar's job. They were betrayed by Kumar and at that time he conveyed upon them the wisdom of India. It was a costly tuition, but Kumar was a teacher of life. Indeed, he was teaching them through negative examples.

One day Kumar got hold of someone completely free of doubt and suspicion.

She was a lady not unlike his own mother. The lady was carrying money. Kumar excitedly started helping her out.

She had lost a son in India. In the week of mourning, she was travelling the same route her son had taken in India. She had come to pray for her son. Her son had written a diary. The previous year, she had been a staff member at the embassy and had no time to slowly see India. Driven by sorrow and having her son's journal in hand, she decided to trace out her son's last steps as a way of reconciling herself.

It was at that time that Kumar appeared. Because of her reason for coming to India, the lady didn't say "Kumar" but started saying "my son" instead.

Kumar had an uncomfortable premonition because every time he was called "son" he would think of his mother in the countryside and recall his family and his pure days of youth.

He vented his anger through swindling, but while he could feel resentment and jealousy toward those the same age as him, to someone his mother's age he just couldn't.

Here was a street of cheap hotels and so there came usually people younger to her age. She was the same age as his mother, so the level of life experience was likewise different. If she had never read her son's journal she would have never come to this street.

His animal-like instinct for swindling dulled. Whenever he was called "son" his feelings for swindling withered.

Finally, he felt like washing his feet and returning to the countryside. He felt like he didn't need the money anymore and that all he needed was to live humbly together with his family. He was homesick.

Attachment as it were, was the most dangerous thing for those amongst Kumar's group. It was a fatal mistake for a professional conman. It suddenly changed his heart to the point that he could no longer swindle someone again for even a second time.

The lady had handed over all her money to Kumar and asked to be taken around. Kumar felt like refusing. Whenever he was called "son" he felt his heart skip a beat. Until now he had been insisting on being the guide, but now it was the opposite. Until now his concern had been how much money he could fill his pockets with, but now from the start, the money was right in front of his eyes. Moreover, he was being called "my son".

Till now he had called travellers "my friend" and "brother" but now he was being called "son" by someone and it jolted him down into his very soul.

On top of that he shed tears for this lady's misfortune of having lost her son and risking her life on this trip. The conman was now conversely having his feelings twisted around.

The lady believed Kumar would guide her back to her son.

It had been his purpose in life to make the doubting people believe, but in this case from the very start he was being believed in. On top of that he was always being called "son" and it made him weep.

After coming to the capital he had been injured, made fun of, scorned, mocked and now his neglected injuries were starting to ache.

It was then that the lady had started to think that this was her real son and she gently patted him on the back. Her love and consideration were so strong that it made a professional conman cry.

It was also the weight of her travel – seeking to trace the footsteps of her son – that placed his timid heart right in front of him.

Her son had been wandering across India for close to a year.

Kumar's trip with her had just started. Kumar no longer thought about a tenfold increase in price. He was cutting the price. The cost of a whole year's trip with her was just barely covered.

She had originally planned to stay for just a month, but upon handing over all her cash on hand to Kumar he admitted, shedding tears, that this was enough to travel for a whole year.

She had already long been divorced and had been living together with her son before. So, she was able to get in touch with her relatives and extend her trip for an entire year.

Kumar's spiritual trip with the lady had just begun. Kumar noticed something. Ethnicity and country might all be different, but the consideration towards one's mother is the same. It isn't some half-way of trusting someone, but an unconscious loving trust like an infant has towards its mother. This wasn't a catch-22 situation nor something one could be deceived by.

He was no longer a swindler nor was he a guide. He was drawn by the spirit of the lady's son and became a pilgrim to various holy sites.

It was then that Kumar understood why so many people came to India and why they were drawn to India.

Though it was inconvenient, dirty, poor and full of swindlers, there were those holy sites and that's why people came. One could entrust oneself to the holy waters of rivers, obtain the blessings of the Gods of the Himalayas and enjoy the compassion of the Buddha.

Kumar's journey of the soul with the lady had just begun.

Comment:

This story is about the swindlers in India. Most of the backpackers travelling in India seek for cheap accommodation and transportation. They are often cheated by such swindlers. This is a common phenomenon even today. In the story I explain this from the perspective of the swindler. Finally, he confesses his wrongdoings. This too actually does happen in real life at times.

Dan's Journey

Dan lived in an underground walkway in Shinjuku in Tokyo. From his childhood he loved making houses out of cardboard. He would make a small house in his room as a kid and played inside it.

Later when he was an adult he worked at a company but unfortunately lost his job and came to actually live in a cardboard house.

Dan lived his life watching those masses of people busily walking about atop the street. Dan didn't hate working – he just didn't have a job. He was already fifty years old and his body was weak. He wasn't able to do manual labour. However, living there in Shinjuku wasn't difficult at all.

He ate food tossed out by restaurants. There were also old clothes to be found. He didn't pay any attention to the scorn and stares of pity from people. If you got past the cops then you could actually manage to live there in Shinjuku. He often thought of how to get along in life with a job, bills and so on. When he quit getting along in life and just started thinking about living, he started living in a cardboard house and lived on the streets.

Dan had his first feeling of actually living when he came to Shinjuku. It was because he was always sitting shoulder to shoulder with death. When he and his fellow residents woke up in the morning it was chilly. The winter mornings were especially cold. Even the young ones had to bear the temperature when it was one degree above zero.

However, mankind for many thousands of years had lived under such conditions and when you stop and think about it, the urban jungle is nevertheless still blessed compared to previous ages.

One day a violent gang showed up looking for some borrowed money and they threatened and beat him up. The next morning everyone ran off and vanished. He thought he might see them in a year, but that was five years ago.

Dan had no idea where his family was and had given up. Even if his family saw him they would not recognize him and would no doubt just pass by. He also didn't want to make his family feel ashamed. At times, the cops would come and take away his cardboard house, so he would have to start all over and rebuild a new house. With this Dan came to discover the real value in his existence in the world. If he himself didn't help out, then everyone would be completely lost on the wayside of the street.

The people walking on the street would either pretend not to see the other people or just pass by. If everyone just ignored them as if they were street lights or mail boxes, then nothing was said. However, it was just the cops who would sometimes actually recognize the existence of homeless people and remove them.

That was Dan's worry. However, unlike stray dogs and cats even if he was taken away he would not be killed and for that he was grateful. But he still knew that the cops saw stray dogs and his kind in the same light. Legally they could kill stray dogs, but not him.

Dan knew he had lost the game of life. In sports and in gambling, there are those who win and those who lose. There were people who for no reason, really scorned those who had lost in life. Dan came to really feel sorry for them.

Still, Dan knew that he was quite blessed having been born in Japan as compared to those unfortunate souls who were starving to death in Africa. That was Dan's sole testament in living. He was born in Japan and was a Japanese. This was the one thing that he would leave behind.

From inside the cardboard house there came sentiments of nationality and a consciousness of ethnicity. It seemed like an idea completely without reason, but for this individual in question it was his only testament to living.

Dan was free the whole day minus having to find some food.

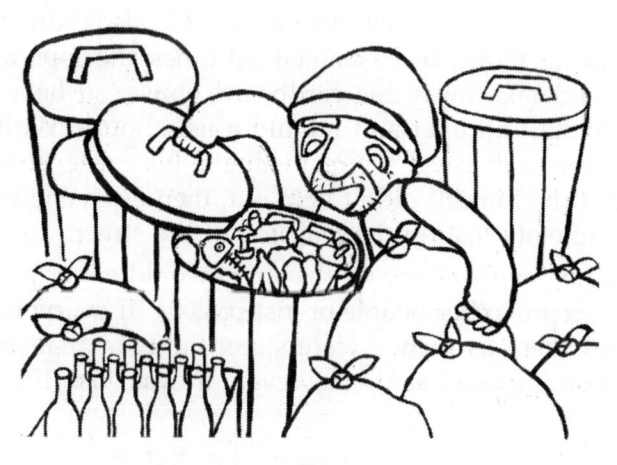

The city was flooded with newspapers, magazines and tabloids. Dan was different from the other vagrants as he used all his five senses and was quite up-to-date on all the latest affairs.

He was unconsciously drawn towards the assets of knowledge. For Dan, who had no money, family or real house to live in, it was something like a divine revelation of sorts. He would pick up the newspaper and spend his time in the day reading it in the park breathing the fresh air. Compared to the people you saw walking the streets and the old air circulating inside some office building, this was actually much nicer. He was able to know all about present events and economic activity just from a rubbish bin. He also knew people's dietary habits better than anyone else just through looking through leftover food.

It was under such conditions and with such luck that Dan became a kind of modern day thinker. Just one look and it was quite clear that Dan's appearance was different from the those of most ordinary people.

Dan would often receive wild applause when he explained these things in terms of economic gaps along with the differences in lifestyle and customs between urban dwellers and tribesmen.

He would explain that they were the original Japanese who were being oppressed. Such people could be traced back to the ancient Jomon period. The younger people in the crowd started to find such an explanation quite agreeable. It was because the young people thought what a jungle the city was with so many people tattooing themselves and dyeing their hair or sitting around on the ground. Nobody could really explain it very well. Sometimes violence would erupt or people would start taking drugs. They started to suffer a kind of complex where they felt they were the ones left behind in society.

People started to become brainwashed by Dan's revelations about why living up in the mountains was good while urban homelessness was bad. His explanations about ancient Jomon period people being reborn in the present day while adhering to old traditions and how such customs conflicted with the modern world.

The natural world which had been so devastated really struck Dan at the heart. That was perhaps also a warning being delivered to humanity who lived in extremely synthetic circumstances quite divorced from nautre. It was perhaps hinting that humanity was for the world a parasite or had become a parasite.

Dan was a vagrant but became a thinker of sorts and the others who felt they had been left behind in society came together around him.

One day just as any other day, when Dan was out looking for food he came across a youth. The youth had been travelling for quite some time and he had run out of cash.

Dan listened to the youth's story and came to realize that by making cardboard houses he was kind of attached to a certain place. As luck would have it the cops showed up and took away his cardboard house again. It was a revelation just like in Hinduism, when at the very end of one's life one sets about to wander for a period of time.

He decided to leave Shinjuku with the youth and to go travel. He had nothing to rely on. Not even a cardboard house. He was completely without any kind of support. Not even a house made of cardboard.

Dan followed his spiritual inclinations and visited various shrines and temples and went to numerous holy sites and mountains. Some people started to look at Dan with respect and reverence.

It was odd because when he was living in a cardboard house, people looked upon him with scorn, but now after having severed his attachments and no longer clinging to a single place while changing his priority to visiting holy sites, he found that people respected him. He was a respected pilgrim all of a sudden.

Just as water produces energy through hydroelectricity or pressure makes the pistons in a car move, Dan changed his direction in life and by wandering from place to place he started walking through life as a new person.

The youth always had a single booklet with him. Every morning he would recite from it. It was a Buddhist *sūtra*.

Dan didn't understand it at all, but seeing the youth from behind reciting it seemed as if he was glowing and it calmed the heart and mind just watching and listening. Dan in such a moment thought that life was like a dream.

The youth noticed Dan in such a state of mind and motioned for him to read it with him. They two recited together. Whether it be in a park or in the mountains or under the eaves of a shop in the market every evening and morning they recited the text.

Dan without really knowing it came to have the appearance of a pilgrim.

In the city he had spent his free time reading newspapers, magazines and comics. Now, he carried with him but one important *sūtra* and every single day he would recite it. Dan was astonished at how different he felt after reading a *sūtra* as compared to a newspaper.

He would first start reciting the text with his voice and then throw his whole self into the recitation. Even though he read the same lines over and over again, he somehow felt that everyday the meaning was different and it became deeper.

Most ordinary things you read are soon forgotten. The meaning and significance also fades with time. It is just like fresh raw food.

However, the *sūtra* the youth had given him when recited allowed an unpolished gem in the depths of his heart to be found and everyday he polished it revealing a beautiful lustre.

Dan realized that the *sūtra* was not really a process of reading as much as it was a process of prayer.

Dan had fallen into homelessness in the city despite having put in a lot of effort in life. He hadn't become lazy or fallen into a life of drugs, booze, womanizing or gambling. For all his effort in life, the one thing he never did was prayed. For Dan in a prosperous period of fast economic growth it had just never occurred to him.

Dan was now starting to consider what exactly he believed in until now. The truth was that Dan had been believing everything that common worldly sense told him. He had entirely put his belief in money, society and salesmen.

So, when he was younger he found work at a small company and upon getting married right away took out a house loan and repayed it his whole life. He had believed the sweet words of the salesman as well as the dream he promised.

Although, his company was often in turbulent circumstances, he believed in his boss' words and continued working reassuring himself that just like a kid who might tumble and fall, everything in the end would be alright and that he himself would become important and great.

He also thought that the bank was supposed to help out those not so lucky. However, he never once thought that the finance company the bank introduced him to would make use of violent thugs to collect their debts. He also had thought his family was of one mind and body with him and never imagined they'd suddenly leave him.

It was due to his belief that if only he protected his house till the very end then somehow he and his family would manage to live that he lost everything.

The idea was that originally when he lost his job and if he sent his family away also didn't upset the gang of thugs he would be allowed to live with his family in a small apartment.

However, the truth is that his house which was tied to a loan wasn't really his house. Japanese society, builders, so-called "common sense" and the banks all sold people a dream of home ownership and for a lifetime had them bound in servitude to repay the debt.

Now, when Dan looked back and thought about it, whatever was he thinking when he signed up for a house loan where he would be repaying the debt until he was seventy years old? Now in retrospect it was ridiculous.

Presently, the earth was his home. He walked the whole earth freely by not owning anything at all. People came to see him with envy in their eyes. The old cardboard house was eventually the same house he had lost before. That's why people used to look at him with pity and scorn. Now, it was different. It was also that now his sense of belief was directed towards the Buddha. He expressed that by venerating *sūtra*.

He recalled reading in some book about this idea of "emptiness" in Buddhism long ago. Now, when he was resting out on the side of highways looking out at the great emptiness of the sky, he realized that this "emptiness" was the greatness that he was looking at in the current situation he found himself in. That was a kind of new testament of sorts that he attained gazing out into the sky.

It was then that Dan felt as if his body was radiating with light and the wind dancing around him. He felt himself ascend into the sky.

It was like being a bird looking down to the earth. He could shift his vision freely anywhere. He was able to see his long lost family. They were living in a corner apartment in some country town close to the sea in a place he had never been before. But rather than feeling a longing for them, he felt as if he wanted to send them loving kindness. Again he shifted his vision and the family faded.

He found he could shift his vision just as simply as changing the gears in a car or using a remote control for the television.

He saw things he had forgotten, things he had once longed for, memories from childhood and people he once had known. It felt like he transcended time and space and followed a path to a mysterious town.

He thought about it and indeed, it was a sight he often saw in childhood dreams, but it wasn't nice at all – he used to feel uncomfortable seeing it and would even wet the bed as a result. However, in real life he had never once stepped foot in such a place.

Even after passing the age of fifty, being able to recollect such strange memories from dreams he had had as a child, was unsettling enough, but all the more when he considered how he would actually find his way there in real life, he was filled with deep emotions.

He was surprised at how the town was just as he had experienced it as a child. This town seemed to tie together the past, present and future. It was Dan's town of the soul. It was a blueprint for his life as well as a kind of internal three dimensional *mandala* of his mind.

Dan shifted his vision again and he was flying through the sky atop snow-capped mountains looking down toward fields of green vegetation. In the distance he could see people wearing white clothes walking in a line toward the light coming from the base of the mountain. Dan wanted to join them, but felt he could not descend from the sky.

Looking down longingly, he met eyes with one of the people who said to him, "As your training is not yet complete, you should once again return to the land. There is no need to be impatient. Anyone and everyone will surely pass through the light and come here and again have a new body. You are being pulled away from here for some reason. First you need to tie up loose ends and then come back!" The character then turned away and faded into the crowd.

Dan had never before heard such a voice echoing into the depths of his heart. It echoed just like *sūtras* did when recited.

He shifted his vision again looking to tie up those loose ends he had been warned about. Again he tried to ascend into the sky but he could not. Though he tried with all his might he just could not. Suddenly, he saw before him the face of the youth he had been travelling with.

The youth looked at him with worry. Dan noticed himself covered in sweat. He had been suffering from a high fever. While looking out at the field across he had fallen asleep not covering himself with a blanket and became ill.

However, thanks to the sweat and visions he had while dreaming, his mood became refreshed.

As Dan started to explain the experience he had had to the youth, the young man suddenly turned into a beam of light and entered his chest. Suddenly, before his eyes a Buddha appeared and spoke to Dan.

"The youth you have been travelling with is a part of me and has been with you until now to protect you. You have fatuously believed everything before your eyes and lived your life as such. However, you, who do not doubt yet always believe are indeed pure in your beliefs. It, is that though you have fallen into ruin, you always have found the light. From herein you must continue your pilgrimage to holy sites and see through the source of whatever is drawing you and continue your practices."

The Buddha then vanished.

Dan was shocked and became silent. He slowly gathered himself and upon standing he felt that his body was lighter. He was rejuvenated and younger looking.

The looks coming from women on the streets were also different. He could move his body more freely and quickly. However, his mind was still wise with age and his experiences were still easily recalled.

Dan considered that back in Shinjuku even if his family showed up they probably would not have recognized him with his haggard appearance. Now he looked much younger and perhaps they still would not recognize him.

The truth is that when you physically become older, your mind also ages. When your mind is rejuvenated so does the body become rejuvenated.

Dan until now had had no thoughts of age appropriateness. That's why he was able to go on a trip with a young person.

Dan now wanted to do something precious with this newly obtained youth. He already knew the limits to worldly pleasures. He was already quite tired of them.

He vowed to use this gift bestowed on him by the Buddha for some great purpose.

What Dan decided to do was to visit shrines and temples. He would pay homage and give thanks for his new found life to all the Gods and Buddha across Japan. Everyday he recited the *sūtra* and called on the enshrined Gods and Buddha.

"Though people are trapped in their lives, bound to money, thinking highly of themselves while slighting everyone else, forgive them. Please accept this prayer of mine. Present day people are just slow at noticing things. Please forgive. I shall make the same prayer all across Japan and the world. Please rescue the world from suffering."

Dan echoed this prayer with him here and there down every street he passed. Dan directed his experiences and strength towards holy aims rather than worldly aims.

It was a beautiful experience of his but not a single one he could convey to other people.

When he travelled in the city, he merely slept on the side of the street. In the countryside he slept under the shade of a tree. His mind was not that of the old Dan. This was Dan, who looked out into the world and prayed for the well-being of all beings.

Even if you initially saw Dan as just another vagrant on the street, you would be suddenly captured by the light in his eyes and the radiance emanating from behind him.

It was through being a homeless vagrant that Dan was able to extinguish the *karma* from his past misdeeds. It was through the scorn of others that he could slow down his rapid aging and hammer a nail into his pride.

Dan's pilgrimage still continues to this day.

Dan indeed continues the pilgrimage that modern people have long forgotten about. Even when his strength expires and he collapses on the street, it still does not end.

He practices wandering just as others have done in India, the homeland of the Buddha. He continues his travels toward the aim of finally reaching that source of light at the foot of a mountain he had once seen in a dream.

Just as when an elephant is about to die it is never noticed by others – it just parts from the herd and proceeds quietly to its own death without the others knowing at all. Likewise with Dan – nobody would ever know of his demise either.

Dan's pilgrimage had only just begun.

Comment:

Due to the enormous recession in the world even Japan as a result has seen the growth of homelessness. However, ancient human beings lived in the jungle and they were not miserable. I try to compare that lifestyle to the modern homeless lifestyle. Should a homeless person have some spiritual purpose in life, he or she has the great potential to become a holy person.

Hathī – The Elephant

In Hindi you call an elephant *Hathī*. Some elephants wander around New Delhi which is the capital of India – the children ride on their backs as they walk around.

India is different from Japan where you don't need to go to the zoo. Elephants, donkeys, cows, horses, sheep, snakes, camels, monkeys and bears all show up in front of your house at some point.

Sometimes without being called they'll even show up at the front porch of your house, ring the bill and invite the children out. Indeed, they're kind of high pressure salesmen for the zoo and playground.

Hathī was just such an elephant with that kind of a job.

Day in and day out he would walk around town with children on his back. He would walk alongside the old man who looked after him. I guess you might say that old man was *Hathī's* master, but in reality when you took into consideration the difference in size, the amount of food *Hathī* ate and how the old man spent so much effort washing *Hathī*, I think you could say *Hathī* was the master.

Hathī's father had a job in the jungle carrying timber. *Hathī's* mother carried bananas. However, with the coming of trucks she changed professions and came to the town to give rides to the kids. *Hathī's* older sister had been recruited into the circus and went overseas.

In India, elephants are Gods. They're kind of living Gods in a sense. So, at wedding ceremonies they're draped in beautiful clothes, crowned with a cap and with the groom, proceed over to the bride's home.

Every month there were many such days and those days *Hathī* felt like a king and was treated like one!

Hathī's best friends were the birds. They would land on him and peck off all the nasty insects. They would whisper in his ear all kinds of gossip. They were friends who would even scratch his itchy feet.

They say the memory of an elephant is greater than that of a human. Even after many years they will remember someone who had harmed them and pay them back for the harm, but on the other hand they also remember good deeds and will always repay kindness.

They can also hear from many hundreds of kilometres away their friends' voices and have a conversation. They also receive information from the birds. They might look a bit dull-witted, but they're actually quite intelligent animals. That's why people respect them as Gods.

Hathī has memories of ancient times. This is something people could absolutely not comprehend and just talking about it would bring about jokes and mockery, but the truth is *Hathī* could remember ancient things from thousands of years ago. People thought him dull and slow, but with the memories well beyond their comprehension he went about his daily walks.

Long ago he was the elephant king of the jungle. When Shakyamuni's mother was carrying him during her pregnancy a white elephant, which was also *Hathī's* ancestor, appeared in a dream and entered her womb foretelling the birth of a marvellous sage.

Hathī was also able at times to remember the age of dinosaurs. It was when he was dozing off during the day that he recalled such times. Dinosaurs had become rather large over time, but because they had acted somewhat selfishly as if they owned the whole world, they became the lizards we know today.

Hathī's ancestors in the age of dinosaurs were the mammoths, but back then, they weren't as large as the dinosaurs. They were quite humble and so until now their form really hadn't changed too much. Nowadays, the lizards can only complain about the glory of their ancestors and maybe look back on it with a bit of fondness.

For both the elephants and lizards they had never even dreamed that humans would control the world as much as they do now, given their rather unremarkable existence in the age of the dinosaurs. As it were, humans now walk the same path of arrogance and pride as the dinosaurs did way back when.

Hathī the former king of the jungle had no other choice now but to work for humans.

The lizards were now completely ignored. In their past they stood out so much that they became chameleons. Put them next to green leaves and they turn green. Put them on brown soil and they turn brown. They try as much as possible now not to stick out so much.

Hathī was well aware that humans were overdoing things to an extreme, but though he might convey it to them, they didn't have the ear to hear it.

So, he entrusted himself to thoughts about the kids and wandered around the neighbourhoods of New Delhi.

Elephants are indeed deities in a sense. They view the world from a perspective that went well beyond the means of humans to measure. There might eventually be a person who understands Hathī's thoughts and convey it to humanity.

If a white elephant should appear in your dream, it might be an omen of sorts. If an echo like the sound of an elephant's foot stomp should be heard, that's also maybe a sign.

Hathī everyday looked fondly back on the past praying with a flower in trunk. You might say that Hathī, the elephant, while not in the jungle, he was the king of New Delhi. However, nobody recognized that so he was the king of a government in exile from the jungle.

Hathī saw all the animals of the world forming an independent country of their own. He was a king with much on his heart and mind. So, he slowly, slowly walked through history thinking back through the times of the past. If you ever come to India, you'll definitely meet *Hathī*.

Comment:

This story introduces how Indian people live together with animals even in urban areas. Elephants are a primary representative of animals in India.

The Plight of India's Mice

In India you call a mouse, *Chūha*. There was once an Indian mouse named *Chūha*. He remembered his ancestors who, some two-thousand five hundred years ago had come weeping when Shakyamuni Buddha passed away.

As you might know, the first of the twelve branches of the Chinese calendar is a mouse.

Also, his friend Mickey Mouse, who the children around the world love very much, was his idol.

However, in order to live, one must eat.

Just nibbling on a single bite of food which humans think of as their own would be met with their anger followed by being poisoned to death or being squashed in a mousetrap.

But then they multiplied like rats as it were and produced many off springs, so they couldn't lose entirely.

Chūha, the mouse had once gone before a sage and vowed in his heart to become a mouse loved by all children. He thought it was his "mission" to be born as a mouse in Shakyamuni's original hometown. Fortunately for him, the people of India thought cats were the servants of demons and disliked them.

The people were keen on eating what they had and so they had nothing extra with which to make poison cakes to kill mice. Their houses were also full of cracks which made it easy to come and go freely. As long as you watched out for snakes and weasels, India was a country so free that you could call it a nation for mice.

Just like how the humans in India were receiving technological support from foreign countries, *Chūha* thought maybe it would be best to study from Mickey Mouse, a kind of celebrity mouse from overseas. *Chūha* knew he was in the same position as him in India. *Chūha* smiled.

Indian people had once had a humble feeling of being able to learn from animals, but recently something went wrong and they learned the idea of multiplying like rats. Before the war there were three-hundred million people and now 1.2 billion! They had really learned well from the mice a thing or two.

Now about his "proposition" to become loved by all children, he really thought about it. It was then that a "thinking mouse" was born. In order to be loved, you have to love others.

Chūha really liked children. He discovered that "really liking" was the way to "really loving" them. However, he had to know well the bitterness of loving others while not being loved by them.

In India, there were many diseases spread by pests and while putting all the poorness of their own sanitation management on the back burner, they started a mass extermination of the mice.

It was then that *Chūha* had the experience of having love turn to hatred. Indeed, love can turn into hatred like a knife through warm butter. Love is the route to hatred.

The mouse, *Chūha* was surprised at the the changes in the depths of his heart. To put his heart back in order he sang a song like this:

"Liking somebody makes you love 'em – *chū, chū... chū!*"

"But loving 'em makes you hate 'em – *chū, chū... chū!*"

Nevertheless, it left *Chūha* feel unsatisfied. He had to have children yearn for him.

The people of India wouldn't kill a single bug. There were also many people who were vegetarian and didn't eat any fish or meat. But because of diseases from pests they had to massacre the mice.

A country at war can easily kill tens of thousands of people.

At this time *Chūha* had no other choice but to throw away his way of thinking where he saw humans as better than his kind.

It was then, that strangely, in his heart he felt some leeway – he had a feeling of pity for humans arise from the depths of his heart.

It wasn't a feeling of "love" so much as a feeling of pity. "How sad... I'd like to somehow help them..." It was warm and genuine.

That was the light of compassion shining forth. It was some two-thousand five hundred years ago that *Chūha's* ancestors had wept before Shakyamuni. That light seemed to shine forth. He didn't have to borrow anything at all from Mickey Mouse – he went beyond just being the loved and adored mouse.

It was in the horror story of the mouse massacre that *Chūha* dug up in his heart, between love and hatred, true compassion.

India's *Chūha* by his own strength is getting closer, one step at a time, to being loved by children just like Mickey Mouse.

Comment:

This story is about discrimination and genocide. Usually, these terms "discrimination" and "genocide" only apply to humans, but they can also apply to animals. This is a basic teaching of Buddhism. It is said that all sentient beings without exception have the potential for Buddhahood.

Kenchin's Soup (Japanese Minestrone Soup)

Long ago in a certain land there was a monk named Kenchin. At a young age he was sent to a temple and there he was trained with all the other monks.

Kenchin was different from the other little monks. He hated studying. However, he absolutely loved wandering through the mountains, gathering wild vegetables, receiving fresh vegetables from the nearby farm and making large meals for the monks in the temple.

He had a big appetite and always enjoyed thinking about food and ingredients. He loved seeing the meals he made and the satisfied faces from those who ate them.

The temple had many monks trained there, so the kitchen was always very busy.

When there was a big *dharma* talk, many monks from other temples would come. At such times it was usually just rice porridge. That was because when the number of people increased you could just add more water and make more.

The temple practiced *shōjin-ryōri* which meant they did not eat meat or fish. Still, because there were many young monks and everyone ate a lot. Kenchin was quite busy everyday gathering ingredients and cooking.

Today, Kenchin had gathered some vegetables and in a corner of the kitchen had peeled them. He then cut them up and was making a side dish.

Tap, tap, tap, tap, tap...

This year there had been a shortage of vegetables and you could not make meals as you might have wanted to. Kenchin sighed looking at the mountain of vegetable peels, tops and tips.

At that time the Spirit of the kitchen stove suddenly appeared. "You don't need to worry! Look around you! You're well looked after. So, you can still eat!" Kenchin was surprised and could not say a word.

This Spirit of the kitchen stove had already been in the kitchen for a long time and it did not seem like he had been really looking after him or anyone else all that well; what with the shortage of vegetables. So, Kenchin worked up the courage and talked to the Spirit.

"This year there has been little rain and hardly any vegetables have been harvested. I cannot bear that the farmers are all struggling and yet they give us so many vegetables. What should I do?" Kenchin got a little sad and started crying. Tears started rolling down his cheeks.

The Spirit, laughed, smiled and wiped away the tears with a gust of wind. Kenchin's tears suddenly turned into sesame seed oil!

Kenchin then hastily gathered the oil in a jar.

"Kenchin! Your kind heart has turned tears into sesame seed oil! Fry up those peels, tops and tips of vegetables over there! Then add some hot water, season it with soya sauce and serve it up to everyone!"

Having spoken, the Spirit vanished into the kitchen stove.

Kenchen then hastily minced the vegetables, made a soup and had everyone eat it. Everyone in the temple was overjoyed. They had returned from a cold meditation hall and filled their bellies with rice and a rich soup infused with the aroma of sesame.

Afterwards in the temple they came to call this soup "Kenchin Soup" and playfully teased Kenchin about it.

The "Kenchin Soup" that everyone knows about came about like this.

It is best not to waste food. It is like the warm compassion of the Buddha.

That's why Kenchin Soup in cold winter days even now still warms people's hearts and bodies.

Kenchin uses every tip and bit of a vegetable and teaches us reverence for life.

Kenchin could not really study and never became a high ranking monastic, but even now he is respected by everyone.

Comment:

This story is about food. Due to deteriorating environmental conditions in the world, food is becoming more and more important and precious. This story tells us how to preserve and not waste any food.

Haruka's Dream

Haruka was born in a remote village of Aomori prefecture's Tsugaru peninsula at the very edge of the main island of Japan.

Her father was always off to Tōkyō working and her mother worked at a Japanese inn in the main city, so being raised by her grandparents she grew up listening to old folk tales.

Overhead of Haruka's village there were always jets flying because of the air route. When the sky was clear and blue the contrails from the planes seemingly sketched things into the sky.

As Haruka grew up she wanted to become a stewardess. She would constantly hear the explosive sounds up above and dream about flying in the sky.

There was a busy air route in the sky between Hokkaidō and Tōkyō, but the Tsugaru peninsula was just completely ignored.

The underground tunnel was definitely the entrance and exit of Honshū. When the tunnel was completed, people just passed by underneath Haruka's village on their way to Hokkaidō. Even though that thick pipe was almost entirely placed above ground, they ignored Haruka's village and had it pass underground.

Haruka's mother had seen the village's youth, all left for Tōkyō as well as after getting married herself seeing her husband went off to work in Tōkyō, so she named her daughter Haruka, which means "far away."

Her mother figured that while she didn't want her to leave, her daughter would still want to leave for somewhere faraway.

However, Haruka's mother had initially told her parents and husband that she wanted to use the Chinese characters for spring scent as she loved Tsugaru's spring time. But because they took too long to write she figured just by putting them in the Japanese alphabet and would make it quicker and easier to write.

The village temple was empty without a resident priest to decide on a name for them. Grandpa, mom and dad had no idea what to do as there was no priest available. After having been at a loss on deciding a name, they were quite happy when they found a name that everyone agreed on. The baby became Haruka.

Tsugaru's spring time was quite beautiful. After being well fed up with the long drawn out winter scenery, spring suddenly came. The villagers all longed for and truly loved spring.

The village was on the coast so there were no apples or rice. It had been Haruka's mother's dream for many years to live and work faraway and she did just that. Grandparents had little interest in leaving, but there were no jobs in the village and after arguing with everyone Haruka's mother left for Morioka.

Haruka's mother longed for distant places, so she named her daughter Haruka, but she herself only went as far as the main city in the prefecture.

During the spring vacation when Haruka became a junior high school student, she ventured out to a rock grotto out on the coast where the leftovers of winter still remained and the voice of raging waves called out. Haruka had been teased by her classmates for being poor at singing, so she had come out to the coast to practice singing.

Haruka, shy and timid, from behind looked very much lonely. Somebody suddenly called out, "Hello! Hello!" Haruka wondered if somebody had just heard her poor singing and her cheeks turned as red as an apple.

The woman had a pure white face. Haruka looked over her shoulder at her with eyes the same colour as her cheeks.

Haruka timidly posed a question, "Where did you come from?"

"Tōkyō."

The woman said just one word and then remained silent.

"What are you doing?"

"Just passing the time."

Haruka wanted to know for what job or what purpose she had come here, but whether it was because her way of asking the questions might have been bad or she had killed the mood she didn't know, but the answers she had been hoping for never came.

At just that time overhead in the pure blue sky the roar of a jet plane echoed and made northward contrails.

Haruka without thinking remarked, "Ah, the jet plane. I also wanted to fly fast like that," and let out a secret she hadn't ever told anyone.

The woman sighed and asked, "What's your dream?"

Haruka leaked her secret and in one breath spilled it all out.

"I want to become a stewardess and fly all around the world. Cuz' you know these planes pass overhead, leave us behind and up above there they draw contrails – they hand out dreams and vanish."

Haruka was able to say that because the woman was a stranger. If she ever told it to the village people, there would have been no way she could receive support to become a stewardess and instead she would have been told to find a job after graduating junior high school or would have been sent to a trade school.

Haruka's eyes were still shining.

The woman looked at Haruka's eyes and then looked up at the contrails in the sky. One could see there was a sudden change in her heart. That woman was actually a stewardess. She had been betrayed by the man she loved, her dreams had been shattered and she thought her life had come to an end. She had come to these cliffs intending to leap into the sea.

However, here was this little girl with apple red cheeks thinking that what she was doing as a stewardess was the greatest dream in life and something to long for.

The job of being a stewardess is actually not a job to long for. Her life was one of irritating customers, jetlag, human interactions inside confined spaces and now lost love, misfortunes and exasperation.

She thought of this little apple-red girl before her and like the leftover winter snow melting her tough heart also started to thaw.

"You know, the truth is I'm actually a stewardess! I was so tired of life and tired of my job – I just finally arrived here..." The woman started to grin at Haruka.

Having been unsuccessful in what she herself had thought to be the greatest dreams in life and having decided to come here and encountering this apple-cheeked young girl, she felt it was her responsibility to teach her that dreams were nothing more than just dreams.

Haruka saw before her eyes a stewardess, who until then was only seen in her dreams. She felt like she entered the highest point of heaven and was confused with various questions.

The woman spoke as if muttering to herself.

"The planes fly, but the people in them don't fly. The space inside the plane stops and it's only time that goes back and forth flying, so really people's minds in the plane don't fly."

She continued, "When an adult gets inside the plane, from the wide seats at the front the adults become spoiled brats! It's like crawling into a mother's womb."

"It's like I'm always a daycare worker or something. If it's a kid, it's cute, but if it's an adult then it's just tiresome. If a kid cries, you just cuddle him or her, but an adult will just get pissed off! So, no matter what I'm saying yes, yes, yes all the time."

"Even though there is a screen in front of passengers explaining the same things, I become the TV aerobics girl. Even though nobody sees you, you give and take away cups and bowls and dance to the announcements. It's like a dance 'for your safety please listen to the following instructions.' It's like the pianist at a rundown hotel where nobody listens to him or the dancer that nobody watches – that kind of grief you experience without thinking about it."

"If you put on an apron, you're a waitress. It feels like a big dining area in a department store. Wine, beer and food on demand – it's an all you can drink and eat buffet. You don't experience that bottomless pit of human desire in the sea... you experience it in the air! If you go up past the front curtain in first class, the waitress becomes no different than a hostess. That curtain is a gateway to sleaze."

"Next is when you become a shop employee selling things at a bargain sale. You walk around with a catalogue and become a consultant. As you push the cart you push the sales. Recently I'm like saleswoman announcing how great this credit card with mileage is! I have to smile cheerfully to make the sale."

"Then we turn off the lights in the plane and put on a movie, and we have a bit of relief. We close the curtain and while standing and almost hiding quickly shovel food into our mouths. Oh, but then some irritating customer will suddenly open the curtain saying, 'Water please! Juice please!' and see us chomping down on our food – it's like they see something they weren't supposed to see and they make this face of complete disbelief. It's a common pattern in old fairy tales: the expression of seeing what you were really not supposed to ever see."

"We're not bloodsuckers or witches – we're youthful little virgins, and though we have big appetites, it is such a shock to see us there hiding and eating."

"It'd be nice if once you put the movie on, people would just quietly watch it, but they push that button to call us. It's the same thing as that button at your bedside in a hospital. Just because they're lonely, they push it and then I feel like a nurse or something."

"We modestly make our announcements with a friendly and beautiful voice, but everyone just yawns and blabbers with each other not listening to us. But that little beep echoes through the plane and the pilot comes on to announce something, everyone lifts their chin up and seriously listens to him. It feels so disrespectful."

"Everyone inside the plane is free to think of it in anyway they please. The people who think of it as a bedroom lift up the armrest on the empty seat next to them and without taking their meal just go to bed. The newly weds are seemingly already in passionate love together in their new home. For those groups led around with a flag it is a celebration hall. It is like in front of a hotel a banner saying, ' Welcome so and so!'. For the moody looking person shifting through documents it is like the president's office, but I'm no secretary. There are people who think it is a three star restaurant. You might look outside and see a dazzling sky of stars, but they just fuss over the three stars.

"Then there's the guy who is like he's being escorted by the police or something and being all downhearted about it. You don't have to be down and cowardly because we're not policewomen. I guess the only thing you can say is that people all have big *karma* in their hand baggage."

Haruka looked at the stewardess, who she had only until now seen in her dreams, and her weary lonely face and felt as if the dream she had, was like a blimp losing its air. She had thought of flying with her body and heart in the sky, but in reality it didn't seem like that was possible.

The lady thought maybe the "medicine" had been a little too effective. In reality, one was really flying or was it just a kind of leaping in life? Thinking about that, flying from place to place and the liberation of one's heart were different things. She wondered if the passage of places on the contrary didn't impede the leaping of one's heart?

She awoke to the reality that the leaping of one's heart toward what you think and what you pray for, what you wonder and contemplate, was really wisdom gained from the experience of travelling in the air so many hundreds of times.

Some time ago she once visited Shakyamuni's hometown in India and spent four days there. When she was there doing nothing in particular she felt a kind of obscurity and which now manifested.

Haruka, right there quickly became an adult. Though she was younger, she became an elder sister. To the migratory bird which shouldered wounds of the heart and rested its wings, she told old stories she had heard from her grandparents.

Haruka was just telling the stories to her as she had remembered them, but the migratory bird had, as if having opened a jewellery box filled with hundreds of years of the villagers' wisdom and realizations, listened intently to Haruka's stories.

Time periods, environments and places are all different, but human lives shine brilliantly as they transcend time.

Haruka from this day onward came to directly see reality. She graduated from a trade school and with the introduction of a guest at her mother's hotel she found a job at a catering service.

It was a job where she sold lunch boxes, coffee and tea from Morioka to Tōkyō. While she couldn't fly through the sky, she was able to fly over the land as if flying through the air.

Haruka was always grinning to the point people thought it somewhat strange. It was because she was doing a very similar job to that stewardess she had helped when she was a junior high school student and knew the job well.

"She is Japan Jet. I am Japan Kitchen. The name is half the same."

"She had to provide meals and drinks for free! I always get money."

"Inside the bullet train adults are adults, children are children. Adults don't become children."

"Because there is no button, I can't be called."

"The uniforms are also quite nice, and they resemble those of a stewardess. The average age can't be compared – here people are younger."

"Tōhoku and Tōkyō have the same time zone. There is no jetlag."

"There are no competitors so even if you're a little blunt with people, it's fine. Those who seem to get angry from the start come to buy lunch boxes and tea from me."

"Those who forgot to bring their lunch or didn't have time to buy one, come to me looking a bit remorseful to buy one."

"Tidying up is done by the passengers and there are also cleaning ladies who come to do it." "If we're running late, the one who apologizes is the conductor. I have nothing to do with it."

In just about every aspect this job was better than what she had heard about when she was a junior high school student. So, every single day she remembered that and grinned.

Haruka was actually quite happy that she never heard any good things from that stewardess. Thanks to having heard those complaints at the time, she was now quite satisfied.

She knew that she made far less money than that stewardess, but nevertheless for Haruka it was a lot.

Then she knew there was the rapid express train to Kansai Airport which was also called "Haruka" and that in her mind she really was flying toward the great big sky.

Haruka had dreams to go far away but her father's love limited the distance to Tōkyō.

Even today that lady and Haruka keep in touch. Thanks to Haruka's stories she has mostly been healed and her heart has likewise been able to fly. She became a kind of mother to passengers. She also imagines Haruka's job and she is able to smile day in and day out.

It's because in her mind she says, "Come on, come on..." while being able to hand out drinks and meals. It's also because she gives to people with a sense of charity and she takes that as her job in life.

Whatever the reality is, it's a job that children all dream about – a job of being able to give dreams. Adults can indeed become children and throw tantrums.

Comment:

Some professions children really admire too much like being a pilot, stewardess, etc... However, each profession has its own problems and difficulties. The dreams of many young girls are often comprised and destroyed when they find out the reality of them. But, if they change their views, they can find a satisfying path in life.

Fortune Pickles and Curry Rice

Everyone probably knows how you put Fortune Pickles on Curry Rice. Have you ever considered why?

It has a real significant meaning. Let's think about it for a minute.

Long ago in Japan in some place there was a poor man. At the river bank he would gaze onto the surface of the river and lived by fishing out garbage from it.

Every year on the night of Bon Festival, the villagers would stick the end of chopsticks into cucumbers and eggplants and come to the side of the river. On pieces of paper they would have their ancestors' death names – special Buddhist names given to them at death – written on slips of paper and float them down the river while praying before returning home. The idea was that the ancestors would ride the cucumbers and eggplants back home like horses. From there when they finished riding the "horses" they would throw them into the river.

It was summer and the poor man, while

absent mindedly staring at the mountain of cucumbers and eggplants, came to think of his ancestors and Buddha. However, at that time he was also very hungry and ate those vegetables which had been used as vessels for long dead ancestors.

He thought, "Oh, I really did eat them all. I really did do something bad! But then the ancestors already left these vegetables behind and returned to heaven, so I wonder if it was okay..."

The poor man got worried. At the time when land was glowing in the light of a full moon, suddenly the Buddha showed up on the opposite bank of the river. The man fumbled for words but couldn't say anything.

The Buddha spoke to the man, "There is value to all the things. So, even those offerings made to ancestors and Buddha, must be used! Use your head! Then, maybe a hundred years from now some strange conditions might come together and ripen into a situation where you are loved by everyone."

The man was so shocked that he couldn't stand up, but then he thought long and hard and concluded, there really was a deep meaning to what the Buddha had said.

He shook his head a moment and tilted it sideways but no wisdom arouse. He suddenly heard a jingle-like noise. He looked down into the water and found a shard of a broken sword. He really had no idea what he was doing, but there on the riverbank in the brilliant light of full moon he started slicing up cucumbers and eggplants with a piece of a broken sword.

Before long as night turned to dawn, there was a mountain of piled up cucumbers and eggplants in front of his eyes.

"What do I do now I wonder? If I don't take them away now they'll go rotten really fast."

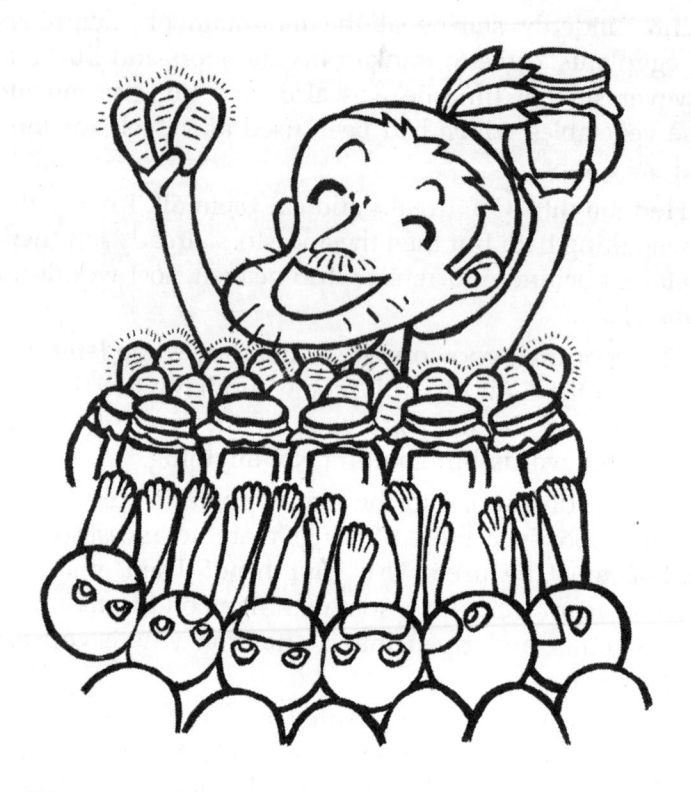

The man thought for a second and came up with an idea. He got together some salt and dyed those ill-fated vegetables into red coloured ones. He thought maybe people might think they were odd looking, so he named them Fortune Pickles while praying to the God of Fortune. When he went to town to sell his pickles everyone was quite pleased and soon they were sold out.

The poor man became wealthy and his Fortune Pickles became cherished by all. However, in his later years he thought about the Buddha's prophecy that in a hundred years something would occur, so he resolved that in a hundred years he would be reborn once more as "Fortune Pickles".

It became the Meiji Period and the Buddha's teachings had declined considerably since the Edo Period. Everyone used to really love Fortune Pickles, but because they were red, it was considered as a thought crime or something and nobody liked them so much anymore.

Everyone had already forgotten the circumstances in which Fortune Pickles had come about.

At the time the English, who were controlling Buddha's home in India, brought curry to Japan. Westerners had initially gone looking for the spices used in curry and had gone many ways to find it resulting in the discovery of the American continent and the conquest of India. It really was an absurd story.

Spice was really that much valued.

The poor man in order to see the Buddha's prophecy, was indeed reborn as "Fortune Pickles".

However, without really thinking hard about it, he had been reborn as "Fortune Pickles" which is not a living being at all; no family, no friends. One is puzzled just thinking about it.

Curry Rice was likewise the same. This dish had come from a faraway foreign land and places on a white plate – it is puzzling. The only thing to relieve the mind of that perplexity is that it had come from Buddha's native place.

It was at such a time that Fortune Pickles met Curry Rice. It was as if they were sharing the Buddha's teaching: Curry Rice from India, Fortune Pickles made at the Buddha's suggestion. The firm relationship was tied together and made permanent. The conversation about the two never stopped as long as the discussion on Buddhism continued.

Afterwards in Japan, the Fortune Pickles were always served on Curry Rice. They were like friends so thanks to fate.

Without knowing it the Buddha's teachings are born in the hearts of Japanese people and in Japanese culture. Buddha loved Curry Rice. So, he might love you too who have ancestors who believed in the Buddha's teachings.

So, those Fortune Pickles, made from the vessels made of cucumbers and eggplants, quietly stare at us from the side.

Like this the Buddha's teachings are very deeply embedded in life in Japan. You never notice that the Buddha protects us from those places.

You might say that the warm feeling that comes from making an offering to your ancestors, perhaps of cucumbers and eggplants, is tied closely to the food of Buddha's home country and it really does make your mouth rejoice as a result. Whenever you eat curry, you might think about these things.

Comment:

Curry Rice is one of the common foods in Japan nowadays. But, it was introduced by the British some one-hundred and fifty years ago. This story is about how Indian Curry Rice is connected with Buddhism. Buddhism, like Curry, came to Japan from India.